Strategic Communications
for Nonprofit Organizations

NONPROFIT LAW, FINANCE, AND MANAGEMENT SERIES

Strategic Communications for Nonprofit Organizations

Seven Steps to Creating a Successful Plan

Janel M. Radtke

JOHN WILEY & SONS, INC.

New York • Chichester • Weinheim • Brisbane • Singapore • Toronto

This book is printed on acid-free paper. ∞

Copyright © 1998 by Janel M. Radtke. All rights reserved.

Published simultaneously in Canada.

Library of Congress Cataloging-in-Publication Data:

Radtke, Janel M.
    Strategic communications for nonprofit organizations : seven steps
to creating a successful plan / Janel M. Radtke.
        p.   cm.—(Nonprofit law, finance, and management series)
    Includes bibliographical references and index.
    ISBN 0-471-17464-5 (alk. paper)
    1. Nonprofit organizations—Marketing—Planning. 2. Advocacy
advertising—Planning.   3. Institutional advertising—Planning.
I. Title. II. Series.
HF5415.R239   1998
658.8'02—dc21   97-32850
                                                                  CIP

Printed in the United States of America.

10 9 8 7 6 5 4 3 2

Acknowledgments

There are many people without whose support this book would not have been written. First, I would like to thank the Robert Wood Johnson Foundation's communications staff—especially Joan Hollendonner, Vicki Weisfeld, and Frank Karel—for their belief in the need for nonprofits to learn communications and for supporting the workshops from which this workbook grew. I'd like to thank *The Training Team*, especially Sally Patterson, Tamar Abrams, and Scott Foote, for constantly challenging me but also supporting my efforts to "get it right." I am especially grateful to Deborah Aubert, whose insights, friendship, and loyalty I've been lucky to have in my life these last several years.

I'd also like to thank Kathryn Edmundson and Karen Menichelli for being there and knowing, back in 1993, that there was something growing out of a half-prepared presentation on a cold day in Chicago. I am forever grateful to my friend Gavin Clabaugh for his patience in teaching me the ins and outs of computers and the importance of defining what it is you're trying to do. I also want to acknowledge my first mentor, Michael Botein, who has given me a motto to live by: figure out what you want to do and we'll find the money to do it. Thanks to Marla Bobowick for helping launch this book and especially to my editor, Martha Cooley, for her patience and her enthusiasm, even when the next chapter was late again.

While there are dozens of friends and colleagues who have stood by me over the years, it is Sherri Eisenpress who has kept me going even when I've wanted to stop. I thank her for being there. I could not have accomplished half of what I've done without her to keep me focused, looking at the bright side of things.

Contents

Strategic Communications as a Way to Effect Social Change

> Too few of those who perform or finance the work that could improve society are alert to the transforming effect of communications. . . . as an institution dedicated to improving mankind's condition, [we] need to attach greater importance to the art of communicating.
>
> Margaret E. Mahoney,
> former president,
> The Commonwealth Fund[1]

Strategic communications is about mission and message. It is about the world in which we live. It is about change of and attentiveness to that world as well. It is the art of expressing our values and our solutions so that people who need to know will *understand* what we are saying. But it is also about the science of transmitting information so that people who need to know will see what we mean and *hear* what we've said.

Many people find today's communications environment intimidating, fast-paced, and chaotic. Often they feel personally and professionally assaulted by today's electronic environment, and many regard technology as a necessary irritation. And, among many people, the mass media are perceived as manipulative, monolithic, and too obsessed with strategy and tactics instead of with issues and understanding.

Our society has more radio stations, television channels, magazines, newsletters, telephones, computers, and fax machines than ever. Nearly two-thirds of our homes receive cable television service and 89 percent own VCRs. Forty percent of all U.S. households own personal computers and millions of people regularly communicate using the Internet. Radios and telephones are everywhere—in our homes, on the streets, and in our cars. People have

---

[1] "Foundations Need Communicators," *NYRAG Times*, Fall 1991, p. 6.

instant access to news, information, and entertainment. Despite all this growth, we seem to have less meaningful communication.

Commercial and for-profit interests overwhelmingly control the images and information that influence our decisions and shape our reality. Advertising relentlessly promotes a culture in which consumption is the solution and every public event promotes private interests. We are no longer citizens first, but rather a nation of consumers.

Technology has altered everything from our personal perception of the world and our relationship to it to how we buy groceries, how we do our banking, and how we entertain, educate, and inform ourselves. With instant news from around the world at our fingertips, the sense that we are living in a global community grows every day. Yet, people lack the sense of common cause, community, and the *public* interest.

What does this mean for nonprofit organizations? Despite the explosion of media channels, it is increasingly difficult to get a message across. There is no "general public" anymore, only targeted audiences, key constituencies, and influentials who, by virtue of their education, income, and activism, have a more powerful impact on public policy than their numbers would suggest. New communications options—which seem to be introduced on a regular basis whether we want them or not—have presented us with dozens of new strategies to consider. Fax broadcasting, e-mail alerts, 24-hour news channels, 800 numbers, infotainment and docudramas have made our jobs more challenging while providing our organizations with new opportunities.

This book is about taking advantage of these new opportunities but not abandoning the tried and true—leafleting, newsletters, direct mail, meetings. It is about a process that is ongoing and constantly in flux. It is about strategic thinking and managing the process so that our organization's goals are realized. It doesn't focus on any one strategy, because a single strategy is not enough to create the change to which we are committed. It is about planning, but it is also about implementation and evaluation. But more than anything else, this book outlines the nuts and bolts of creating a communications plan. This is because organizations survive by conducting their day-to-day business at a practical level; they thrive when that business is infused with mission, vision, and values. This book attempts to cover all the bases in a way that everyone—whether they consider themselves "communications professionals" or not—can understand and use.

The other purpose of this book is to help grant makers understand how integral communications is to the success of the programs they fund. There is a growing sense in the philanthropic community that *communicating is important.* Hopefully, this book will show just how important it is. When a grantee practices strategic communications, a foundation's grant is leveraged because the impact is greater than it would have been without that communications component. A grant maker at a large foundation once remarked that the foundation's guidelines required organizations to explain how they plan to communicate the results of their program. He estimated that approximately 80 percent of all grantees failed to address the issue in their proposals. Yet, this omission had never stopped that foundation from making a grant. While that fact alone says volumes, the frame of reference here—communicating the *results* of the program—is wrong. Organizations are in the communications business—and that means it is not only about *what happened* but also about *what is happening, what we want to happen, and why.* Communications efforts cannot occur after the fact; they must be ongoing, woven into the fabric of the programs to which the organization and the foundation are committed.

Communicating is about building understanding. It is about nurturing change. When we enter into a conversation with someone, we are changed by it. When a national tragedy like the Oklahoma City bombing occurs and we not only watch television coverage or read news accounts but also discuss the matter with friends and colleagues, we are changed. When an issue is discussed and decided on at a community board meeting, we are changed. When we attend a rally, read a book, or participate in an audioconference, we are changed. Social change, political change, *change* is the business of the nonprofit community.

Many organizations and consultants have struggled to define strategic communications, but, like many things, we know it when we see it. We know it helps advance program objectives within the context of the environment in which we live, and, in many cases, the environment we are trying to change. We also know that it is a skill of great importance in our media-driven world. But do we know how to do it?

This book is more about learning how to communicate strategically than providing a philosophical construct for a debate about what strategic communications is. It is hoped that you'll learn to "know it when you see it" even if you can't define exactly what it is.

Getting the Most out of This Book

The idea behind this book is to help you create a communications plan for your organization. With this in mind, there are several tools in addition to the text to guide you through this process.

Tips, Guiding Questions, Checklists, and Rules of the Road: These lists provide practical advice to help you critique your work and shape your ideas. They are based on lessons learned through years of experience by many communications professionals.

Worksheets are provided in each chapter to assist you in developing the information you need for each step along the way. They complement the text and should help you structure and focus the thought process involved in each step. Blank worksheets are included at the end of each chapter as well as on the disk included with this book.

Finally, while some of the organizations used to illustrate various components of a communications plan are real, several—Planet 3000, Shelter from the Storm, and Future Generations—were created by combining various aspects of real organizations and are fictional.

Strategic Communications
for Nonprofit Organizations

Step #1:
Why Invest in a
Communications Plan?

To Advance the Mission

A mission statement has to focus on what the institution
really tries to do. . . . The mission is something that
transcends today, but guides today, informs today.[1]

EVERYTHING IS MISSION-DRIVEN

Every organization has a mission, a purpose, a reason for being. Often the
mission is why the organization was first created—to meet a need identified
years ago. The question we need to ask is, "Does the mission still address
issues that are of concern in today's world?"

Sometimes, the same problems the organization initially tried to address
haunt generation after generation and an organization's purpose doesn't
change—although how it does business very likely has evolved. Other times,
even ten or twenty years can change the landscape so markedly that the original mission must be updated, modestly altered, or changed dramatically to
address those new realities.

That your organization's mission is current, alive, and well, however,
doesn't necessarily mean that the organization has translated that purpose
into a clear, concise mission statement. A good mission statement should
accurately explain why your organization exists and what it hopes to achieve
in the future. A vital mission statement also articulates the essential nature of
an organization, its values, and its work. This should be accomplished in a

---

[1] Peter F. Drucker, *Managing the Non-Profit Organization,* 1992, pp. 4, 141.

brief paragraph that is free of jargon or terms that are shorthand with others who work in the field but may not be readily understood at first glance by "the average person"—people who are outside the organization or the field in which it works.

Another consideration is how recently your mission statement was reviewed by board or staff members. If it was more than five years ago, you may be facing a golden opportunity to ensure the relevance of your organization by reviewing and, if necessary, fine-tuning or even rewriting your mission statement. All too often an organization's mission statement, which has been handed down over the years, has lost its vitality and ceases to elicit passion among staff, board members, and supporters. Yet the mission statement is what the organization must use to "rally the troops." Because of this, it must resonate with the people working in and for the organization as well as with different constituencies the organization hopes to affect. It must express the organization's purpose in a way that inspires commitment, passion, innovation, and courage—not an easy task!

At the very least, your organization's mission statement should answer three questions:

1. What are the opportunities or needs that we exist to address? (the *purpose* of the organization)

2. What are we doing to address these needs? (the *business* of the organization)

3. What principles or beliefs guide our work? (the *values* of the organization)

Here are three mission statements that answer these questions. Let's look at what they have in common and why they work.

1. The mission of Big Brothers/Big Sisters of America is to make a positive difference in the lives of children and youth, primarily through a professionally-supported One-To-One relationship with a caring adult, and to assist them in achieving their highest potential as they grow to become confident, competent, and caring individuals, by providing committed volunteers, national leadership and standards of excellence.

   • *The purpose*: to make a positive difference in the lives of children and youth so that they'll achieve their highest potential

   • *The business:* providing and supporting committed volunteers who have one-to-one relationships with children and youth

- *The values:* individuals who are confident, competent, and caring; leadership and standards of excellence

2. The National Conference, founded in 1927 as the National Conference of Christians and Jews, is a human relations organization dedicated to fighting bias, bigotry, and racism in America. The National Conference promotes understanding and respect among all races, religions and cultures through advocacy, conflict resolution, and education.

   - *The purpose:* to fight bias, bigotry, and racism in America

   - *The business:* advocacy, conflict resolution, and education

   - *The values:* understanding and respect among all races, religions, and cultures

3. Planet 3000 is committed to healing the earth. Using research into natural ecosystems, Planet 3000 develops policy recommendations and pilot projects that apply these underlying principles to human ecosystems such as cultural habits, social structures, commercial ventures and the like. It advocates for the establishment of human ecosystems that are in harmony with other life on the planet. By bringing the human social order into balance with ecological principles, diversity of all living things can be sustained and the evolutionary process that has guided and nurtured life on this planet for millions of years can continue unabated.

   - *The purpose:* to heal the planet

   - *The business:* advocacy, research, and demonstration projects

   - *The values:* ecological principles, balance, diversity, the evolutionary process, and harmony with life on the planet

Tips for Writing Mission Statements

1. Your mission statement should act as the organization's guiding light, pointing the way toward the future.

2. Your organization's purpose should be expressed in an emotional way in order to inspire passionate support and ongoing commitment.

3. Your mission statement should include a vision of the future that is possible, articulated in a way that is easy to understand and 100 percent convincing.

4. Your mission statement should articulate the organization's values in such a way as to be the motivating force behind everyone connected to the organization.

5. Your mission statement should use proactive verbs to describe what you do.

6. Every mission statement should be jargon-free and expressed in language that could be easily understood by an eighth-grader.

7. Your mission statement should be short enough so that anyone connected to the organization can readily repeat it when asked by anyone else anywhere at any time.

Forms to help you create a mission statement can be found on the CH0101.DOC disk.

THE SITUATIONAL ANALYSIS

Periodically, every organization should conduct a situational analysis—sometimes known as an environmental scan. The purpose of a situational analysis is to help key players within your organization know as much as possible about the internal and external environment in which your organization exists—for better and for worse. The more you know about the environment in which your organization is working, the more effective you'll be in communicating your message. The situational analysis should be a written document that is updated on a regular basis—at least once a year.

A comprehensive external situational analysis should have three components.

1. The *public environment*—which groups of people or organizations have an interest in the activities of your organization: whether that interest is for or against doesn't matter. They have a stake in what it is you do and they have an impact—or the ability to impact—your organization (see Exhibit 1-1).

2. The *competitive analysis*—a list of groups that compete for the attention and loyalty of the publics identified. These organizations often are viewed as competitors because financial resources, whether they take the form of grants, fees, or individual donations, are limited. The competitor organizations may provide similar services to similar audiences, or they may be *perceived* as doing the same things your organization does—whether that is true or not.

Exhibit 1-1. *Publics* That Might Be Connected to Your Organization in Some Way

---

❑ Colleagues at other organizations
❑ Organizations that have similar program interests and values
❑ Organizations that oppose your work
❑ Organizations with whom you partner
❑ Clients
❑ Activists/advocates
❑ Board members
❑ Volunteers
❑ Private foundations
❑ Corporate foundations
❑ Donors
❑ Community leaders
❑ Community groups
❑ Church groups
❑ Reporters, editors
❑ Government officials/policymakers
❑ Nongovernment policymakers
❑ Local media
❑ National media
❑ Parents
❑ Educators/teachers
❑ Corporations—senior managers
❑ Small business owners
❑ Children (K–12)
❑ Youth
❑ Health care providers
❑ Social service agencies' staff
❑ Others _____

Once you've created a list of publics connected to your organization, define them succinctly and write a sentence or two to describe their connection to or investment in your organization and its work.

Begin with the organizations you've already listed in your public environment scan. To hunt down additional information that may not be as apparent or known to you, your staff, or your board, you can use the following resources:

- Directories, such as the *Encyclopedia of Associations* or the *Association Yellow Book,* are available at most libraries. They provide information about the purposes, memberships, and budgets of not-for-profit groups.

- The Internet: search using key words. Just remember to be as specific as possible in your search, so that you don't have to scroll through 10,000 entries!

- Colleagues, funders, and editors of trade publications can provide names of organizations that do similar work. You can then contact those organizations for information.

By the end of this process, your staff and board should be able to decide which organizations have agendas and audiences that overlap with yours. You should also be able to "grade" these competitor-colleagues as (1) truly competitive, (2) somewhat competitive (and in what areas), and (3) not really competitive. This exercise also will help you identify how your organization might collaborate with others to leverage limited resources, learn from each other's experiences, or avoid duplication of services to identical populations.

3. The *macroenvironment*—the outside forces that shape opportunities and pose threats to the organization. By researching five primary areas, your organization can prepare itself to take advantage of opportunities these forces present as well as have ready contingency plans to avoid or lessen the impact of any threat set off by one or several of these five factors. Examples of outside forces to look at when doing a macroenvironmental scan:

Demographics. A shift in the population you serve—getting older, having children, moving to other communities, absorbing an influx of immigrants—could bring about new demands on resources, a shrinkage of services and staff, or a new group of volunteers or activists for the organization.

Economic. The perception of the economy will have an impact on the level of giving by individual donors, while the actual economic factors will affect the level of resources available for foundation and corporate giving.

Economic indicators may also suggest the need for higher levels of existing services; new service opportunities; or a constituency in the making for a specific public policy position.

Technological. Advances in technology can create cost-effective ways to relate to different audiences, do research, track grants, and compile and analyze information.

Political. Political decisions impact almost every nonprofit organization one way or another. One has only to look at the impact of health care or welfare reform, communications deregulation, environmental policy, or foreign aid to see how intricately interwoven the fates of nonprofits and foundations are with the political environment.

Social. Changes in the social agenda or cultural norms can affect an organization either positively or negatively. The impact of home schooling on education, and the growing awareness of society's responsibility in areas such as drinking and driving, domestic violence, or safe sex, influence which strategies will be most effective for nonprofits to pursue.

While these forces are not controllable by any one organization, each organization has a vested interest in staying abreast of developments and, when possible, influencing those developments in ways that will help the mission and not hinder it. But we must know what these forces are before we can figure out an appropriate response to them.

The best way to keep abreast of these five areas is to stay informed not only about current affairs—through newspapers, specialized publications, and news services—but also to conduct informal discussion groups every six months or so. Such discussion groups can help to either confirm or challenge the general perceptions of staff members as to where these five forces are heading and what impact to expect and/or plan for. Indeed, this is a great exercise to use to solicit the best thinking of your board of directors in a way that can be truly useful in moving the organization forward.

 Exercise #1: Using the forms provided on the disk, draft an external situational analysis for your organization. Remember to include information on the public environment, the competitive environment, and the macroenvironment.

A situational analysis that focuses on the internal workings of the organization is often called an *internal audit*. It looks at the organization's culture and structure, program and management objectives, human and financial resources, and physical and technological infrastructure. By examining these pieces of the puzzle, the staff and board should be able to understand not only what is possible but also what is permissible given this set of facts.

For example, an organizational structure that has worked for the last 25 years may no longer be appropriate given the need for interdisciplinary teams. The administrative structure itself may have to change in order to achieve the desired results—for example, the flow of information and setting work priorities among interdisciplinary teams, members of which come from several different departments with different supervisors who have different priorities, may require a reconfiguration of those departments and/or their responsibilities.

Along the same lines, an organization's culture will influence how extreme or how cautious it will be when planning its strategies, having a strong affect on what is permissible. The morale of the staff will have an effect on its commitment to new programs. When an organization's management objectives conflict with its program objectives—for example, cutting over-head versus expanding the program—the reconciliation of these two facts will dictate what is possible within the organization. If the organization is financially sound, it may be able to do more. And, if the organization under-stands how to maximize the technological infrastructure already in place, it will be able to work more cost-effectively.

Specific areas that need to be reviewed during the internal audit process follows, with questions to help guide your thinking as you get ready to do your own internal audit.

Organizational Culture

- Is the organization conservative and cautious or more liberal and experimental?
- How much autonomy does the staff have in its work?
- Is there a desire on the part of the board to build partnerships with other organizations?
- How is staff morale?
- Do staff members naturally help each other with problems they encounter, or is there a feeling of "that's not my job"?
- What is the energy level at the organization on any given day?
- Is there a relatively free flow of information within the organization or do people believe that "information is power" and thus hesitate to share it?
- What is the attitude at the organization? Open and friendly? Scared and paranoid? Cynical?

- Does everyone feel comfortable offering their ideas to others for discussion and consideration?
- Do staff members feel that they are treated fairly?

Organizational Structure

- Who reports to whom?
- What departments work together on which programs?
- Are there any interdepartmental teams that meet on a regular basis?
- Are there any areas where responsibilities overlap?

Program Objectives

- Are they reasonable?
- Do they address the needs of the external environment (as discovered during the external situational analysis)?
- Can they be prioritized or are they all of equal importance?
- Which publics (from the external situational analysis) will be affected positively or negatively by each objective?

Management Objectives

- Is staff aware of the management objectives of the organization?
- How do the management objectives relate to program objectives? Do they help or hinder?
- Has the organization defined what each management objective means and why it is important for the organization's success?
- How are management objectives decided on? Is there any input or feedback from the staff?

Human Resources

- What expertise does our staff have?
- What knowledge base does our staff have?

- Do we have a good mix of program and line staff?
- Do we have sufficient staff to meet our objectives—for example, how often do staff members work overtime?
- Do we provide training to our staff?
- Do we have staff expertise in all the areas on which our organization is focused?
- Do we have too many or not enough volunteers for the programs that require volunteer involvement?
- In addition to leadership, does our board of directors contribute to the organization a mix of skills—financial management, fundraising, public relations, legal, program-related, and so forth?
- Does our staff include one or more *recognized experts?*

Financial Resources

- Is the organization breaking even?
- Does it pay its expenses in a timely manner?
- Does the organization have a reserve fund?
- Does the organization rely on any revenue-generating products or services for a substantial portion of its budget?
- How much has the organization grown over the past three years? Has it been a steady growth pattern or one with many ups and downs?
- Does the organization have a core group of supporters on whom it relies—both foundations and individual donors?

Physical Infrastructure

- Does the organization have enough work space for staff, consultants, and temporary workers?
- Is the space conducive to teamwork?
- Is there adequate light, air, and heat?
- Can people have a private conversation if they need to?
- Is the building in a safe neighborhood—will staff feel comfortable working odd hours if needed?
- Is there room to expand if we take on new programs?

Technological Infrastructure

- Do the people who need computers for their work have them on their desktops?

- Do we have the necessary software to do what we need to?

- Is there an adequate number of phone lines so that callers don't experience a busy signal?

- Should we network our computers to facilitate the sharing of information between staff members?

- Are we maximizing the use of our printers? Our telephone system?

- Do people know how to use their computers? Their phones?

- Do we have a fax machine? Is it time for another?

- Do we have access to a VCR and monitor? To a video camcorder?

- Does the staff do a lot of conference calling? Is it worth buying a phone made especially for conference calling?

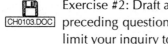 Exercise #2: Draft an internal audit for your organization. Use the preceding questions to guide you through the process, but don't limit your inquiry to these questions; rather, use them to stimulate questions of your own.

DEFINE YOUR PROGRAM GOALS

Once you are clear about your mission and can state it in a brief paragraph, and you understand the environment in which your organization is working, you're ready to develop program goals for your organization. This is what you hope to accomplish over time. Your goals define how your organization will actualize its mission. Goals are the outcomes that guide your organization's activities, project decisions, and management functions. They provide the backbone for its program activities. Most goals are long-term—several years—and provide organizations with a "big picture" from which to design specific programs.

A program goal should answer two questions:

1. What impact or change do you want to happen?
2. Who will you serve or influence by doing this?

These three program goals have been effective guideposts for the National Institute for Dispute Resolution and demonstrate how open and broad program goals can and should be.

1. To build infrastructures at the local, state, and national levels that support the universal teaching—and practice—of non-violent conflict resolution throughout our schools and neighborhoods.

2. To equip community stakeholders—elected and appointed officials, members of community-based advocacy and nonprofit service organizations, business leaders and individual citizens—with conflict resolution skills so they can create socially, economically, and environmentally healthy communities.

3. To foster sound public policies in response to the challenge of decentralized decision-making by expanding states' capacity to use conflict resolution processes such as regulatory negotiation, facilitated public dialogue and public policy mediation.[2]

Organizations can also have what might be considered internal, management, or functional goals as well as program goals. While these may not seem directly related to your organization's mission, they can play a critical role in its ultimate success and may impact the allocation of your communications resources. An example of this type of goal setting:

1. To maintain accurate and current financial information that is easily accessible to key staff and board members so that they can maximize the impact of the organization's financial resources at all times.

2. To develop and nurture an enthusiastic, committed, and well-informed staff and board.

Tips for Goal Setting

1. Your organization's goals should grow out of your mission.

2. They should have a long-term, big-picture focus.

3. When put together, they comprise an organizational "wish list."

4. A goal is the end result your organization wants to achieve.

5. Every goal should specify what you want to happen and who will be affected by this work.

---

[2] As described in the National Institute for Dispute Resolution 1996 Annual Report.

CLARIFY YOUR OBJECTIVES

Each goal will have several program objectives that quantify and qualify that goal into manageable "chunks." Program objectives identify benchmarks that can be used to evaluate your effectiveness and to ensure movement toward eventually achieving each program goal. These objectives lie at the heart of an organization's program strategies and project activities. They will also be used to formulate doable communications objectives from which your communications plan will emerge.

Whenever possible, program objectives should include a realistic target date for completion. The number of people or percentage of the targeted audience by which you'll measure your success should be specified. If money can be used as a measurement, there should be an amount—whether in dollars or as a percentage of a current benchmark—that you want to reach. An objective should state exactly what you hope to accomplish with those people or that money.

Unlike program goals, objectives are limited in scope and evolve over time. When one is fulfilled, it usually leads to the development of another and another before an overall program goal is achieved. Often program objectives build on the work of previous program objectives, creating momentum for the overall program goal. The key to creating effective measurable objectives is to be as specific as possible.

An example of an objective without measurements might be:

Create awareness within the community of the effects of alcohol on teenagers.

To turn this into a measurable objective, five areas need to be clearly defined:

1. Area of change
2. Direction of change
3. Target audience
4. Degree of change
5. Time frame or target date

Given these criteria for developing program objectives, one possible way to rewrite this objective might be:

"To increase the understanding of all parents in School District 20 about the effects of alcohol on the learning capacity, self-esteem, and health of our youth by convincing 50% of these parents to become involved in Parents Fight Back by July 1, 1998."

1. Area of change   Understanding of alcohol's effect on teens

2. Direction of change   To increase

3. Target audience   Parents in School District 20

4. Degree of change   50% become active in Parents Fight Back

5. Time frame/target date   July 1, 1998

With specific benchmarks in place, it is possible to develop appropriate strategies and programs to achieve the objective as well as to measure progress. The ability to evaluate how close we are to the targets we've set pro-- vides critical information that can be used to (1) fine-tune and refocus our efforts when necessary, and (2) effectively build on our success.

Tips for Developing Program Objectives

1. Always set a target date to indicate when you want to accomplish the objective.

2. Specify the degree of change—either in numbers or percentages of an existing figure—that can be counted and/or measured along the way.

3. Identify the population within which you want to create the change.

4. Clearly state what it is you want to accomplish and create ways to put measures around it.

5. Ask yourself what would have to happen—what would have to be manifested—to indicate that something has been accomplished with this group of individuals.

CREATING COMMUNICATIONS OBJECTIVES

A communications objective focuses first and foremost on the audience and what you will do to engage audience members or get them to change, partic- ipate, and become involved in helping you achieve your program objective. It is a fine line and one that is often not apparent to the unpracticed eye. It includes measures similar to regular objectives but looked at through a slightly different lens:

1. The target audience
2. The nature of the change among that target audience (direction of change)
3. The specific knowledge, attitude, or behavior to be achieved (area of change)
4. The amount of change desired (degree of change)
5. The target date

Sometimes a program objective can serve as a communications objective. From Planet 3000's program plan:

> To educate community leaders and youth in six communities about different ecosystem principles in order to build consensus for possible public policy recommendations.

1. The target audience
   - Community leaders and youth in six communities
2. The nature of the change among that target audience (direction of change)
   - To educate
3. The specific knowledge, attitude, or behavior to be achieved (area of change)
   - Ecosystem principles
4. The amount of change desired (degree of change)
   - Consensus on public policy recommendation
5. The target date
   - Over the next year

The direction of the change—to educate—must entail some sort of communicating, as does consensus building. The program objective is all about communications, and it will involve a number of different communications strategies and tactics that are appropriate to the target audiences.

At other times the program objective must be analyzed further to find the underlying communications objective. Our earlier program objective illustrates this situation.

> To increase the understanding of all parents in School District 20 about the effects of alcohol on the learning capacity, self-esteem, and health of our

youth by convincing 50% of these parents to become involved in Parents Fight Back by July 1, 1998.

1. The target audience
   - Parents in School District 20
2. The nature of the change among that target audience (direction of change)
   - To increase
3. The specific knowledge, attitude, or behavior to be achieved (area of change)
   - How alcohol affects youth
4. The amount of change desired (degree of change)
   - 50% join Parents Fight Back
5. The target date
   - July 1, 1998

"To increase" does not convey a communications objective. The question to ask to clarify the communications objective would be *how* will we increase this understanding. There are many ways, several of which are listed below.

- Inform all parents in School District 20 about the effects of alcohol on their children.
- Explain to all parents in School District 20 the purpose of Parents Fight Back and the time commitment it would take to participate.
- Discuss the need for active participation in Parents Fight Back and the difference these parents' participation would make.
- Convince 50 percent of these parents to join Parents Fight Back.

One way to test for a communications objective is to consider the verb in the sentence. Does it reflect a communications activity? Some verbs that naturally indicate a communications objective include:

Educate

Teach

Inform

Provide

Conduct

Enlist support

Mobilize

Sign up

Discuss

Promote

Build consensus

Like a program objective, a communications objective will have at least one audience group identified. When a communications objective has several audience groups, it may be easier to have a single communications objective for each individual audience group.

Finally, communications objectives often are differentiated by the nature of the intended change and the specific knowledge, attitude, or behavior to be achieved. For example, the first level of communication might be to simply inform someone about something. To educate someone about that same thing takes more effort and results in a more active or committed audience member. To advocate or promote something to someone is likely to fall somewhere between informing and educating. To mobilize or convince someone to do something might be considered the next level of communications activity. So, while all of these activities involve *communicating*, they each serve different purposes and require different strategies.

Indeed, it may be useful to look at communications objectives as a cyclical process (see Exhibit 1-2)—when you reach the end, you are once again at the beginning. Each quadrant builds on the one before. Once you have someone's attention and have created an awareness of the situation, you can begin to engage their thinking about it and/or initiate the relationship. At this point they are more likely to act (whether or not they are asked to do so by you). The final stage is maintaining and strengthening the relationship. This can lead back to the beginning of the cycle—for example, making activists aware of pending legislation or informing volunteers of a new mentoring program.

Tips for Creating Communications Objectives

1. Analyze the verb used in your program objective. Does it relate to a communications activity?

2. While studying your program objective, consider who you need to do what, then what you need to do to get them to do that—for example, educate, inform, promote, advocate.

Exhibit 1-2. The Communications Process

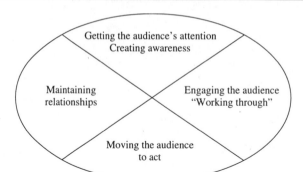

3. Think about the reasons we communicate with different people or groups of people. What is it we hope to achieve by engaging in that communicating behavior? Now look at your program objective and consider the same question.

4. Remember to clarify—as much as possible—the nature of the desired change and the specific knowledge, attitude, or behavior to be achieved.

In short

The mission focuses on *why* your organization exists.

The situational analysis focuses on *where* your organization exists.

The goals focus on *what* your organization wants to make happen.

The objective focuses on *how* your organization will make that happen.

The communications objective focuses on *who* needs to be reached and *why*.

 Exercise #3: Goals, program objectives, and communications objectives

1. Write out the goals of your organization.

2. List at least three program objectives that you want to achieve within the next year. Preferably, each goal should have at least one objective. Remember to be as specific as possible.

3. Under each program objective, create at least one communications objective. This will become the foundation for your communications plan.

MISSION STATEMENT WORKSHEET

Put any words, phrases or ideas that people have with respect to the organization and these various categories. Do not edit at this point. Give everyone's voice a chance to be heard.

Purpose: Why We Exist

1. Opportunities:

2. Needs:

3. Problems:

The Business of the Organization

1. How are we responding to the opportunities?

2. What do we do to address the needs/ problems?

(Continued)

The Values of the Organization

1. What are our organization's principles?

2. What does our organization stand for?

3. What values guide our organization's staff and volunteers?

Write the mission statement based on the language and concepts that had universal agreement as outlined above. Remember that it should be no more than five sentences.

Mission Statement:

Check Your Work:

❏ Does it point toward the future?

❏ Is it expressed emotionally?

❏ Will it cause passionate support?

❏ Will it inspire ongoing commitment?

❏ Is the vision of the future possible?

❏ Is the vision easy to understand and convincing?

❏ Will the values motivate everyone connected to the organization?

❏ Does the statement use proactive verbs to describe what you do?

❏ Is there jargon?

❏ Could it be understood by an eighth-grader?

❏ Would someone be able to repeat the gist of it when asked what the organization was about?

CH0102.DOC

THE SITUATIONAL ANALYSIS

1 = truly competitive
2= somewhat competitive in these areas
3 = not really competitive

Publics That May Be Connected to Your Organization

Category/name	For/against	Reason for connection	Competitive status

*Place a check in front of those organizations
with whom your organization might collaborate*

Colleagues at other organizations

☐ _____	F A	_____	1 2 3
☐ _____	F A	_____	1 2 3
☐ _____	F A	_____	1 2 3
☐ _____	F A	_____	1 2 3

Organizations with similar program interests and values
Organizations with whom we partner

☐ _____	F A	_____	1 2 3
☐ _____	F A	_____	1 2 3
☐ _____	F A	_____	1 2 3
☐ _____	F A	_____	1 2 3
☐ _____	F A	_____	1 2 3
☐ _____	F A	_____	1 2 3
☐ _____	F A	_____	1 2 3
☐ _____	F A	_____	1 2 3
☐ _____	F A	_____	1 2 3

Organizations that oppose our work

☐ _____	F A	_____	1 2 3
☐ _____	F A	_____	1 2 3
☐ _____	F A	_____	1 2 3
☐ _____	F A	_____	1 2 3
☐ _____	F A	_____	1 2 3
☐ _____	F A	_____	1 2 3
☐ _____	F A	_____	1 2 3

☐ Clients	_____
☐ Activists/advocates (for us)	_____
☐ Activists/advocates (against us)	_____
☐ Board members	_____
☐ Volunteers	_____

Private foundations

☐ _____ F   A   _____ 1 2 3
☐ _____ F   A   _____ 1 2 3
☐ _____ F   A   _____ 1 2 3
☐ _____ F   A   _____ 1 2 3

Corporate foundations

☐ _____ F   A   _____
☐ _____ F   A   _____
☐ _____ F   A   _____
☐ _____ F   A   _____

☐ Donors   _____
☐ Community leaders   F   A   _____
☐ Community leaders   F   A   _____

Community groups

☐ _____ F   A   _____ 1 2 3
☐ _____ F   A   _____ 1 2 3
☐ _____ F   A   _____ 1 2 3
☐ _____ F   A   _____ 1 2 3
☐ _____ F   A   _____ 1 2 3
☐ _____ F   A   _____ 1 2 3
☐ _____ F   A   _____ 1 2 3

Church groups

☐ _____ F   A   _____ 1 2 3
☐ _____ F   A   _____ 1 2 3
☐ _____ F   A   _____ 1 2 3
☐ _____ F   A   _____ 1 2 3
☐ _____ F   A   _____ 1 2 3

Reporters, editors, media outlets, specific programs

☐ _____ F   A   _____
☐ _____ F   A   _____
☐ _____ F   A   _____
☐ _____ F   A   _____
☐ _____ F   A   _____

Government officials/policy makers

☐ _____ F   A   _____
☐ _____ F   A   _____
☐ _____ F   A   _____

(Continued)

☐ _____ F   A   _____
☐ _____ F   A   _____

Nongovernment policy makers
☐ _____ F   A   _____
☐ _____ F   A   _____
☐ _____ F   A   _____
☐ _____ F   A   _____
☐ _____ F   A   _____

☐ Parents   F   A   _____
☐ Educators/teachers   F   A   _____
Corporations – senior managers
☐ _____ F   A   _____
☐ _____ F   A   _____
☐ _____ F   A   _____
☐ _____ F   A   _____
☐ _____ F   A   _____

Small business owners
☐ _____ F   A   _____
☐ _____ F   A   _____
☐ _____ F   A   _____
☐ _____ F   A   _____
☐ _____ F   A   _____

☐ Children   F   A   _____
☐ Youth   F   A   _____
Health care providers
☐ _____ F   A   _____ 1 2 3
☐ _____ F   A   _____ 1 2 3
☐ _____ F   A   _____ 1 2 3
☐ _____ F   A   _____ 1 2 3
☐ _____ F   A   _____ 1 2 3

Social service agencies' staff
☐ _____ F   A   _____ 1 2 3
☐ _____ F   A   _____ 1 2 3
☐ _____ F   A   _____ 1 2 3
☐ _____ F   A   _____ 1 2 3
☐ _____ F   A   _____ 1 2 3

Others

❏_____ F A   _____ 1 2 3
❏_____ F A   _____ 1 2 3
❏_____ F A   _____ 1 2 3
❏_____ F A   _____ 1 2 3
❏_____ F A   _____ 1 2 3
❏_____ F A   _____ 1 2 3
❏_____ F A   _____ 1 2 3
❏_____ F A   _____ 1 2 3
❏_____ F A   _____ 1 2 3
❏_____ F A   _____ 1 2 3

List somewhat competitive organizations and indicate how they compete:

Name   **How They Are "Somewhat Competitive"**

_____   _____

_____

_____   _____

_____

_____   _____

_____

_____   _____

_____

(Continued)

Examining the External Environment

Demographics: *Has there been a shift or change in the populations or the makeup of the communities you serve?*

If yes, what does that mean? If no, is that cause for alarm?

Economic: *How do donors perceive the economy and what does that mean for our financial future?*
Will the economy impact the funding available from private foundations?
Is the economy shifting in ways that will cause a growth or a decline in demand for services from the populations we serve?

Technological developments: *What are the latest trends in business technology that we might use to become more cost-effective? What are the latest products or trends in technology that could impact our program areas of interest – health delivery, social services, job training, education, etc? How will these trends impact our organization? Can we afford to apply this technology to create a better product, provide improved services, conduct more cost-effective advocacy efforts?*

*Political: What do we expect to be on the national, local, and state political agenda this year? Could it affect our organization or the populations we serve? If the winds blow our way, what can we expect? If they go against us, what's the worst that can happen? Is there something we're **not** seeing?*

Social: What social or cultural trends are we seeing in the community, in the state, in the nation? What does this mean for our organization and its work?

What social or cultural values do our constituents subscribe to? Have these values changed recently? If so, why? Does that impact our relationship to our constituents?

What is the "mood" of the nation? Our community? What's the latest fear in society? What's the latest demand? What's the latest "hope" or "solution" being talked about? How could these fears, demands, and hopes impact our work?

THE INTERNAL AUDIT

The questions your internal audit must examine are on the left. Write your thoughts on the right, alongside the questions to create whole paragraphs about each area you examine.

Organizational Culture   **Write Here**

- Is the organization conservative and cautious or more liberal and experimental?

- Is there a desire on the part of the board to build partnerships with other organizations?

- How much autonomy does staff have?

- How is staff morale?

- Do staff members naturally help each other with problems they encounter, or is there a feeling of "that's not my job"?

- What is the energy level at the organization on any given day?

- Is there a free flow of information within the organization or do people see information as power and hoard it?

- What is the attitude of staff and volunteers? Open and friendly? Scared and paranoid? Cynical?

- Does everyone feel comfortable contributing their ideas?

- Does the staff feel that it is treated fairly?

Organizational Structure

- Who reports to whom?

- What departments work together on which programs?

- Are there any interdepartmental teams that meet on a regular basis?

- Are there areas where responsibilities overlap?

Program Objectives

- Are they reasonable?

- Do they address the current needs of the external environment?

- Can they be prioritized, or are they all of equal importance?

- Which publics will be affected by this objective either positively or negatively? How will their response impact the organization?

Management Objectives

- Is the staff aware of the management objectives of the organization?

- How do management objectives relate to program objectives? Do they help or hinder?

(Continued)

- Has the organization defined what each management objective means and why it is important for the organization's success?

- How are management objectives decided? Is there any input or feedback from the staff?

Human Resources

- What expertise does our staff have?

- Do we have a good mix of program and line staff?

- Do we have sufficient staff to meet our objectives – for example, how often do staff members work overtime?

- Do we provide training to our staff?

- Do we have staff expertise in all the areas on which our organization is focused?

- Do we have too many or not enough volunteers for the programs that require volunteer involvement?

- In addition to leadership, does our board of directors contribute a mix of skills to the organization – for example, financial management, fundraising, public relations, legal, program-related, etc.?

- Does our staff include one or more *recognized experts*?

Financial Resources

- Is the organization breaking even?

- Does it pay its expenses in a timely manner?

- Does the organization have a reserve fund?

- Does the organization rely on any revenue-generating products or services for a substantial portion of its budget?

- How much has the organization grown over the past three years? Has it been a steady growth pattern or one with many ups and downs?

- Does the organization have a core group of supporters on whom it relies – both foundations and individual donors?

Physical Infrastructure

- Does the organization have enough work space for staff, consultants, and temporary workers?

- Is the space conducive to teamwork?

- Is there adequate light, air, and heat?

- Can people have a private conversation if they need to?

(Continued)

- Do staff members feel comfortable working odd hours if needed?

- Is there room to expand if the organization takes on new programs?

Technology Infrastructure

- Do the people who need computers have them on their desktops?

- Do we have the necessary software to do what we need to?

- Is there an adequate number of phone lines so that callers don't experience a busy signal?

- Do we need a LAN or Intranet to facilitate the sharing of information between staff members?

- Are we maximizing the use of our printers? Our telephone system?

- Do people know how to use their computers? Their phones?

- Do we have a fax machine? Is it time for another?

- Do we have access to a VCR and monitor? To a video camcorder?

- Does staff do a lot of conference calling? Is it worth buying a phone made especially for conference calling?

How will this information help or hinder us in the year ahead?

PROGRAM GOALS AND OBJECTIVES WORKSHEET

Tips for Goal Setting

1. Goals should grow out of your mission.
2. They should have a long-term, big-picture focus.
3. Do they represent the organization's "wish list"?
4. The goal should specify what your organization wants to happen and who will be affected by it.

Tips for Program Objectives

1. Set a target date.
2. Give numbers or percentages of an existing figure that can be counted and/or measured along the way.
3. Identify the population within which you want to create the change.
4. Be specific about what it is you want to accomplish and put measures around it.
5. What would have to happen to indicate that something has been accomplished with this group of individuals?

Goal #1

```



```

Specify objectives to make goal happen.

Objective #1

Area of change: _____

Direction of change: _____

Target audience: _____

Degree of change: _____

Time frame: _____

Write objective #1.

```



```

Developing Communications Objectives

Communications Objective #1

Target audience: _____

Nature of change among target audience: _____

_____

_____

Specific knowledge, attitude, or behavior we want to achieve: _____

_____

_____

Amount of change desired: _____

_____

Target date: _____

Write your communications objective here.

_____

_____

_____

_____

_____

CHAPTER TWO

Step #2:
Who Can Make It Happen?

Identify and Know Your Audience

Every organization is swimming in a sea of publics.[1]

Who among this mass of people represents the groups that
they really should be talking to?[2]

HOW PUBLICS EMERGE

How often have people expressed a desire to "reach the general public" or "do a public education campaign"? What do they mean by this? As the "general public" numbers over 5 billion people, trying to reach everyone seems silly at best, certainly not strategic, and definitely not something most organizations can afford! This is why it is critical not only to identify your target audience(s)—or "public(s)"—but to learn as much as you can about them in order to achieve success in your communications endeavors. An organization's actions have consequences for other organizations or groups of people. It is through this consequential relationship that organizations create publics. Publics are formed when people face a problem, recognize that the problem exists, and organize to do something about that problem. When we combine these two factors, the consequences of an organization's action may affect some publics in a positive way while at the same time having a negative impact on other publics. The tobacco wars give us a clear example of how this

---

[1] Philip Kotler, as quoted in Peter F. Drucker, *Managing the Non-Profit Organization*, 1992, p. 76.
[2] VALS senior research psychologist Bruce MacEvoy, as quoted in R. Piirto, *Beyond Mind Games: The Marketing Power of Psychographics*, 1991, p. 76.

works. Public health organizations want to stop people from smoking in order to prevent sickness and death. The consequence of their action for many publics will be better health. The consequence of these same actions for tobacco growers, however, is economic uncertainty.

PROBLEM RECOGNITION

The aware and active publics share the fact that they *recognize the problem.* For this reason they are more likely to seek out and process information, creating a fertile environment for an organization's communications effort. Yet, if people from these same publics perceive obstacles or constraints in a situation that seem to place limits on their freedom to act or to plan for their future, they are less likely to seek out and process information. Communication with these people is thus more difficult, because they feel powerless to effect a change.

1. *The latent public:* People who face a common problem but fail to recognize it. Communication with these people is difficult because they don't realize there is a problem. However, they shouldn't be ignored: When the problem is finally recognized, this public could quickly become a problem for an organization.

2. *The aware public:* People who recognize that they have a common problem. An organization is most likely to be effective in communicating with this group.

3. *The active public:* People who organize to do something about a problem. They generate consequences for organizations. Often, active publics discount an organization's communication because they tend to use alternative information sources to reinforce attitudes already constructed.

Two other types of problem recognition can help us understand our audiences and how they will respond to our communications efforts:

- Internal problem recognition is an intellectual awareness of a problem that piques curiosity and stimulates understanding as an end in itself.

- External problem recognition is a pragmatic recognition of a real-world problem requiring a real-world solution.[3]

---

[3] Dozier and Ehling, "Evaluation of Public Relations Programs," In James Grunig (Ed.), *Excellence in Public Relations and Communications Management.* Hillsdale, NJ: Lawrence Erlbaum Associates, 1992, p. 174.

LEVEL OF INVOLVEMENT WITH THE ISSUE

The next thing to consider is the level of involvement your audience feels—that is, the extent to which they connect themselves to a situation or issue. The more closely connected an audience feels to a situation, problem, or issue, the more active individuals will be in seeking out information and actually processing it. Grunig and Hunt, in a 1984 study, pointed out how level of involvement with an issue translates into different publics:[4]

- *Activist public:* Highly involved; these people relate to many issues and feel they can do something about the recognized problems.
- *Apathetic public:* Individuals who are uninvolved and fatalistic about issues.
- *Universal-salience public:* Generally apathetic except about issues that directly affect nearly everyone in the population.
- *Single-issue public:* Individuals highly involved with one issue and apathetic to others.

There are many reasons for someone to get involved with an issue. Sometimes the involvement is ego-driven—these individuals are resistant to changing their attitudes and, while they are likely to actively communicate, it is usually to support existing attitudes. At other times, individuals feel like an issue has significant personal consequence. These individuals are likely to develop reasoned and well-founded attitudes. They objectively evaluate incoming communication to elaborate on information already received. People who feel that an issue has some—but not a lot of—personal consequence are less concerned with the quality of persuasive arguments, think less about the issue, and depend on cues such as source credibility to develop attitudes.[5]

PUTTING THEORY INTO PRACTICE

Now you can look at the target audience groups—also referred to as publics, constituencies, or stakeholders—noted for each of your communications objectives. At the same time, you will want to identify other publics—individuals, groups of people, organizations, agencies, businesses, and so on—

---

[4] J. E. Grunig and T. Hunt, *Managing Public Relations.* New York: Holt, Rinehart & Winston, 1984.
[5] Dozier and Ehling, p. 174.

who can help you either achieve those objectives or influence your primary audience. Label each group by its connection to the organization in the particular situation the objective defines.

By occupation	Teachers, nurses, actors, engineers, scientists, policy makers
By shared experience	Parents, widow(er)s, illiterate or unemployed adults, dropouts, runaways, people living in the same neighborhood
By common relationship to your organization	Activists, volunteers, staff, board members, clients
By the benefits to be gained from association with your organization	Members, chapters, donors, coalition partners, corporate funders—both foundation and marketing staff

Remember: How you identify these groups may change as you gather information about the individuals who make up each audience. In fact, a single audience group may become several smaller, more precisely defined groups to whom you'll target your communications effort.

For example, within the donor audience there are high- and low-dollar donors. They act in different ways financially, yet both support the organization and its mission. Donors usually are segmented by specific criteria. Each group of donors should be approached in a way that speaks directly to its needs and desires. This allows the organization to maximize its communications with individuals who make up these segments in its attempt to influence behavior, attitudes, and/or opinions.

A useful caveat from Daniel Yankelovich is to never assume one segmentation will work best. Consider all possible segmentations, then choose the most meaningful based on what you are trying to do or have done.

While there are occasions when an organization's key audience may be an audience of one—a key funder, a policy maker, or the chairman of the board—it is more likely that the organization will need to communicate with many individuals or groups simultaneously. But it is also just as likely that it will need to focus its attention on a few key audiences before expanding its effort to other audience groups. This staggered approach can maximize resources while at the same time creating the momentum needed for long-term success. For example, you may need to enlist the support of local school boards and principals for an in-school health clinic before you can begin communicating with parents and students about the clinic and why they should support it. Obviously, if the school board rejects the proposal for the clinics, the message sent out to parents and students may be very different—"Tell the school board you want the clinic"—than what might be said if the clinic gets the go-ahead from the school board—"We're happy to announce that your children will have a place to go when they get sick or have an accident at school."

As previously mentioned, other audience groups may not be the primary target of your organization's objective but may be important because they have contact with or influence over members of the target audience. These "outreach partners" can help you reach your key audience, often more cost-effectively than trying to reach those key audience members directly. For example, if a clinic wants to provide prenatal care to 50 low-income women each month, it might solicit help from social service agencies, pregnancy testing centers, low-income housing associations, or homeless shelters to reach the women who are most in need of these services instead of mounting an extensive (and expensive) consumer media campaign. In the same way, if your organization has worked hard on health care reform and a bill has finally made its way to the governor's desk, it may be more useful to examine your organization's high-dollar donor list or board of directors to see who has a connection with the governor and have that person deliver the organization's message rather than the executive director or a small group of volunteers. The more specific you can be when defining your key audiences and potential outreach partners, the easier it will be to find the most effective ways to communicate with them.

GETTING TO KNOW YOUR AUDIENCE

It's apparent by now that it isn't enough to simply identify key audiences. The next step—and the more difficult task—is to learn all you can about them so that you can "stand in their shoes" and relate to their point of view. Ideally, you want to be able to say that you honestly know what individuals from each audience are like; what makes them tick; what problems or prejudices they have; and what they think and feel about your organization, issues, or services as well as the larger world in which they live and through which they will experience your organization, its work, and its message.

First, jot down the audience group you've defined as a top priority for your first communications objective. List the members' habits, interests, and activities, their shared experiences, cultural attitudes, values, personal beliefs, and opinions. What adjectives describe them? What's important to them in their lives? What motivates them to do what they do? Look at what you already know—or think you know—and write it down. Try to picture a real person—someone you know—that embodies this audience (or perhaps is an actual member of the audience). Write his or her name down as a way to jog your memory when working with this audience. This connection to a real person will help you reinforce the idea that the larger audience is composed of individuals just like "Joe."

All too often we harbor assumptions about certain audiences that may not be true. Not challenging these assumptions at the outset could lead to ineffective messages, inappropriate strategies, unmet objectives, and wasted resources.

There are many tools that can help make this more than a simple guessing game. Some are expensive—individualized market research studies, polling, or psychographic reports such as *The Monitor*, which is produced by Yankelovich, Clancy and Shulman and sold to subscribers for tens of thousands of dollars.[6] But other methods are affordable and doable—you just need to know what information you're looking for. Then a little time, and perhaps a small amount of money to cover the cost of phone calls, postage, printing, media subscriptions, and access to the Internet, will be in order.

Audience Segmentation: The Basics

There are three types of information usually used to segment audiences: demographic, geographic, and psychographic. Other audience characteristics that can be used to help target audiences have to do with the power to influence those audiences or the desired outcome:

- *Covert power:* Who has the power to influence decisions in an unexpected or "unofficial" way?

- *Position:* Who has power by virtue of status in an organization or community?

- *Reputation:* Who is described by others as knowledgeable or influential on a given issue or in a specific community?

- *Membership:* Who has power because of their connection to the organization?

---

[6] Yankelovich, Clancy and Shulman, Inc., 8 Wright Street, Westport, CT 06880, (203) 227-2700.

Demographics: Vital Statistics of Human Populations

In the United States, demographic information is gathered primarily by the U.S. Census Bureau. This data, obtained from the Bureau, is manipulated and analyzed by researchers for a variety of reasons—everything from unemployment statistics and public health indicators to public transportation planning and market research. How you use demographic information to understand your audience(s) will depend on (1) which categories of information are critical to connecting with your audience and (2) the time and money you can spend to obtain and analyze demographic information that already exists (see Exhibit 2-1).

This is just the tip of the iceberg, but it makes the point as to why demographic information is important to use in defining your audience. As you think of other reasons, note them on the worksheet at the end of the chapter.

It quickly becomes evident from the information in the right column that certain preferences and wants often become associated with demographic variables. This is not simply conjecture or generalization. Research has shown that the predictability of various preferences and wants within specific demographic sectors is surprisingly accurate. Because of this, demographic factors are a way to help you "get into your audience's head" and its experience of life.

Each individual experiences certain milestone events—such as marriage, the birth of children, separation or divorce, children growing up, or the death of a spouse or parent—that not only mark the beginning and ending of different phases of life but also change the experience of life forever. When certain demographic factors are combined—most notably age, marital status, presence of children, and whether an individual lives with parents or independently—a picture of a person's life begins to emerge.[7]

Geographics: Where People Live

Geographic information tells you where your target audience lives, which in turn will say much about how it experiences the world. Where a person lives—in a city, suburb, small town, or rural setting, in a wealthy, middle-class or poor neighborhood—will have an effect on his or her attitudes, opinions, habits, and perceptions. In addition, people from different states or regions of the country often share characteristics with others in their own

[7] J. Walter Thompson researchers studied these variables and created a proprietary service, "LifeStages" which has nine categories ranging from At-Home Singles to Young Parents to Mature Singles to Empty Nesters. For more information, see Piirto, pp. 104–109, or contact J. Walter Thompson at 466 Lexington Avenue, New York, NY 10017, (212) 210-7293.

Exhibit 2-1. Demographics

Demographic category	Some reasons why it makes a difference
Sex	"Men are from Mars, women are from Venus."
Age	A 10-year-old is concerned about braces, a 20-year-old is concerned with fitting in; a 35-year-old woman is concerned that her biological clock is running down; a 45-year-old woman is dealing with perimenopause.
Income	A family of four with an income of $25,000 worries about paying the bills; a family of four with an income of $60,000 wonders how they'll save for the kids' college.
Education	More college-educated men than men with a high-school education have computers in their homes.
Marital status	A single person is looking for a special someone to share his or her life with; a married person is working on building a relationship—leads to different choices on how to spend time and money.
Occupation	Shapes our day-to-day experience of the world. It is affected by economic cycles. Bus drivers spend 8 hours on the road; store clerks spend their shifts behind a counter; construction workers spend theirs outside while lawyers, doctors, business professionals spend 12 or 15 hours inside buildings, sometimes never seeing the light of day. The magazines they read are different. The time spent watching TV is different.
Race	People of different races look different. The result is that lines are drawn (redlining for mortgages, affirmative action, voting districts), a shared culture and community grows within those lines, fear of the difference triggers hostility, and wanting to see past the difference leads to misunderstandings and community building.
Family dwelling location	City life versus suburban life versus life on the farm—different pace, different air, different views.
Family size	Whether we have no children, an only child, or a family of 7 influences how we relate to the world.
Life cycle	The lives of young couples who are recently married tend to be centered on their careers, while young parents tend to focus on their children.

regions, but not necessarily with others who live in the same kinds of settings in different regions. An easy way to understand this is to consider the attitude toward education or crime of someone living in a suburb of Los Angeles. It is very likely that another person living in the suburbs of Chicago, Seattle, or New York has a different attitude or opinion about the same issues, even though he or she shares a suburban lifestyle and, perhaps, income level with the person from Los Angeles.

Think about the difference that geography makes in how people grow up, what they experience, what they value, what they are surrounded by (see Exhibit 2-2). Add to your worksheet as ideas come to you.

Geodemographics: You Are Where You Live

This type of segmentation is done by looking for the average demographic characteristics of a particular geographic area and applying them to everyone in that area—for example, a neighborhood, a zip code, or several blocks. The geographic area—commonly known as a "cluster"—becomes defined by the demographic characteristics of the average person in that neighborhood. While these systems are based on demographic information, they have also been tied to psychographic data and media usage studies. The result is that

Exhibit 2-2. Geographics

Geographic category	What difference it makes
Country	The United States is not Mexico Different culture, government, economy
Region	The Northwest is not the Southwest Different sensibilities, economies
State	New York is not California; South Dakota is not Florida Climate, regulations, economy
City	Miami is not Dallas; Milwaukee is not Chicago Pace, culture, politics
Zip code	Congressional districts
Neighborhood	Considered home Stores, parks, restaurants, families, friends
Rural	Traveling 60 miles to town is not unusual
Town	Each has its own unique center
Suburb	Homes, strip malls, and giant stores

each cluster is given a more detailed picture. Of course, there will always be exceptions within a geodemographic cluster—individuals who are not like the people among whom they live.

Perhaps the best-known geodemographic system is Claritas' PRIZM (Potential Rating Index for Zip-code Markets), which categorizes the United States into forty lifestyle clusters. Mark Weiss' *The Clustering of America* presents and explains how clusters are used to define audience segments, creating a portrait of the American population as consumers that can be used to better understand various audience groups. If you've defined your audience geographically, but may not have easy access to demographic data because it may be too costly or time-consuming, this type of information can provide a general insight into the attitudes and media habits of the average person living within your defined geographic areas.

Psychographics: Analyzing the Individual

"Psychographics is the use of psychological, sociological, and anthropological factors, such as benefits desired, self-concept and lifestyle to determine how the market is segmented by the propensity of groups within the market—and their reasons—to make a particular decision about a product, person, ideology or otherwise hold an attitude or use a medium."[8]

The three basic psychographic categories are:

- Activities—how people spend their time
- Interests—what's important to them in their immediate surroundings
- Opinions—how they view themselves and the world around them

Psychographics is the final piece of the segmentation puzzle and perhaps the most elusive to grasp. It looks at how people perceive themselves and the world around them by considering values, attitudes, and lifestyle. While this type of information can be invaluable in understanding what motivates people to do something or influences their opinion or perceptions, it is also very expensive to gather and requires the skills of an expert market researcher or polling group to be done correctly. However, it is useful to know what psychographics is. Should your organization choose to conduct in-depth interviews or survey a sample of a key audience group, you may want to consider including questions that reflect the concerns of several psychographic categories enumerated in the following list.

---

[8] Emanual Demby, as quoted in Piirto, p. 18.

A detailed framework for audience analysis first published in 1974 remains an excellent ready reference tool for anyone involved in understanding audiences.[9]

Activities	Interests	Opinions	Demographic
Work	Family	Themselves	Age
Hobbies	Home	Social issues	Education
Social events	Job	Politics	Income
Vacations	Community	Business	Occupation
Entertainment	Recreation	Economic	Family size
Club membership	Fashion	Education	Dwelling
Community	Food	Products	Geographic
Shopping	Media	Future	City size
Sports	Achievements	Culture	Stage of life cycle

The implications of psychographic information are readily seen. Because there are so many areas on which it is possible to concentrate, it is best to pick several that are key to your objective and your issue and/or that will point to something unique about members of your audience—something that differentiates them from other audiences yet connects them to your organization, or that could suggest possible communications strategies. For instance, hobbies might not seem relevant to a nonprofit organization and its issues. Yet amateur gardeners might be a key audience to target for an environmental objective.

IMPLEMENTING YOUR AUDIENCE ANALYSIS

Obviously, there are many ways you can categorize and define an audience using some or all of the information above. Now that you know what type of information you're looking for with respect to your target audience, it's time to figure out how best to gather it. While this can be a time-consuming process, it will be time well spent, and in the long run it will make your communications effort more cost-effective.

[9] Piirto, p. 27. Framework designed by Joseph Plummer in the *Journal of Marketing*, January, 1974.

While market research techniques are most effective when practiced by experts who know how to ask the right questions, manipulate data, and analyze statistical models, the information readily available in the marketplace can help anyone learn more about target audiences and gain valuable insight into their attitudes, opinions, and media preferences—useful information when working on a communications plan.

A list of different tools and techniques is provided below. Choose one or combine several, depending on the time and resources available to you. Finally, some techniques may be more appropriate if your audience is identified as *individuals*, while other tools may be more useful if your target audience is made up of organizations where organizational participation and not necessarily the participation of a group of individuals is desired to achieve a program objective—for instance, coalition building. The most important caveat to keep in mind as you decide what techniques or tools to employ in gathering information and using it to analyze your key audiences is: *Use techniques you're comfortable with.*

Media Review

Observe and read everything you can—books, government reports, academic studies, analyses of census data, periodicals, online information. Study popular culture, music, and literature. Monitor online discussion groups that focus on topics of interest to your organization. Watch for trends. Pay attention to polling done by local or national media. Take time to do online searches—use your key audience group category as a key word for the search. (For more on *media reviews,* see Chapter 3.)

American Public Opinion Index

Published annually by the Opinion Research Service in Boston, MA, this index is a comprehensive listing of all the studies done during the year—a menu of "who's asking what of whom." The in-depth version—on microfiche or CD-ROM—also contains what was said. When you find a study of particular interest, you can contact the researcher for more information and, in many cases, get at least a summary of the research findings. The *index* can be found in many libraries and may provide you with detailed information that you previously thought was unavailable to you.

Questionnaires

Many organizations conduct written surveys of newsletter readers or donors. The three issues to consider are choosing a representative sample of your key audience to receive the survey; developing clear questions; and (an often-overlooked step) making sure you get a high response rate. The easiest way to choose a representative sample assumes you have a database that includes members of the audience group you are targeting. You can select everyone—if it is a small group—or choose every third, fifth, or tenth person from the list. Next, make sure your questions (1) get to the heart of the information you need to learn about the attitudes and motivations of your target audiences and (2) cannot be misunderstood or misinterpreted by audience members. It is best to develop questions with at least two people and to informally test them on others—family members or friends—to ensure that each question is clearly understood and elicits the information you need. Finally, commit staff or volunteer time to call nonrespondents or ensure that your budget can accommodate second and third mailings. Sometimes offering an incentive—whether with the survey or "to the first 100 respondents"—can be useful in getting people to respond. (For more on surveys and questionnaires, see Chapter 7.)

Piggybacking

Several national research organizations regularly conduct omnibus surveys that combine questions from a number of sponsors. Look into the possibility of adding a few questions to these surveys. This can be a very cost-effective way to get information from a national or regional sample.

Polling

Using a market research expert to conduct a public opinion poll can be an expensive proposition—one that may only be affordable if your organization combines its resources with those of other organizations interested in the same audiences or the same issues. However, you might try to recruit a local academic who has an interest in your organization's issues to help you with this type of research. Or, alternatively, you might introduce the possibility of examining the public's opinion on a given topic during an editorial board meeting so that the newspaper covers the cost of the poll.

Interviews

Sometimes the best way to find out what members of a target audience are thinking or why they do what they do is to ask them. There are numerous ways to conduct an interview, but the most important aspects of this approach are the questions asked and the ease with which the interviewer handles the interview. In addition to the tips outlined in the section on **questionnaires,** for interview questions you need to use the method that will be used in the actual interviews—either face-to-face or phone—to test the validity and clarity of the questions.

Mall Intercepts.   These are short, on-the-spot interviews where staff or volunteers ask several questions face-to-face in a public space—frequently this is done at shopping malls where individuals are "intercepted" and asked to take a few minutes to respond to key questions. But intercepts could also be done outside office buildings, on college campuses, at the grocery store, on a playground, or on a downtown street. The idea is to go to the place where members of your key audience are likely to be and elicit their reaction to your concerns.

In-depth Interviews.   On the other side of the spectrum are in-depth interviews where people spend anywhere from an hour to ninety minutes asking questions that probe the reasons people do what they do or think what they think. Often interviewees are visited in their homes—or in a neutral setting without emotional overtones—so that they feel relaxed and less threatened by the in-depth nature of the questions.

Phone Interviews.   Interviewing individuals over the phone is another way to collect information directly from members representing your key audience groups. This is done successfully by numerous market research firms or can be undertaken with the help of staff and volunteers. In order to maximize response, it is useful to call first to schedule an agreed-on interview time and not simply to assume that the current call is convenient for the recipient. Interviews don't have to be at one end of the spectrum or the other. They can include as many or as few questions as you like and the questions can be either multiple-choice, yes/no, or open-ended. However, the longer the interview, the more likely people will self-select out of the interview. Remember: The time and place of the interview—whether you call someone at home or at work, in the morning or evening—may influence the answers given.

Focus Groups

According to Judith Langer, president of Langer Associates, the success of a focus group depends on the design of the questions, the skill and training of the moderator, the careful selection of the panelists, and the correct interpretation of the resulting conversation.[10] Many organizations bring together representatives from key audience groups to engage in an informal conversation about issues or services. While these informal discussions may be useful in gleaning the attitudes of these particular audience members, they are not necessarily focus groups. In addition, the opinions expressed by the individuals gathered may not necessarily translate to a larger audience group. (However, any dialogue with representatives of an audience group is likely to be beneficial and enlightening.) One of the benefits of this approach is that you can elicit responses from several people at once. One of the drawbacks is that the opinions of one or two may influence others unduly and, most likely, only temporarily—that is, while they are sitting in the group. A single attitude or opinion may be concurred to by the group yet not be truly reflective of the individual opinions.

If you want to conduct a formal focus group, it is probably best to find a trained moderator—either a paid consultant or a professional moderator who will volunteer for the job. However, if you do want to proceed with an informal discussion and get the most benefit from it, you should choose someone to moderate the discussion who can "listen with a third ear, watch the body language, and pursue leads that lift the corner of the blanket."[11] (For more on focus groups, see Chapter 7.)

Ethnography

This technique consists of simply observing people in action—actual behavior can speak volumes. Often the easiest way to find out why people do something is to observe them doing it, then ask them about the circumstances surrounding their actions. Obviously, this method won't be appropriate for every audience group. But it can be a useful tool with specific audiences around specific topics—for example, high school students smoking or individuals donating blood.

---

[10] Piirto, p. 134.
[11] Piirto, p. 134.

Create a Picture

Once you've gathered enough information about a specific audience group, begin building a human profile of one individual in that group. What does he or she look like? Who does he or she have relationships with and why? What does an ordinary day in his or her life look like? Give the person a first and last name. Or, if you prefer, use a real person you know or who you've met to represent the essence of the audience group for you as you move forward with your plan. Giving an audience group a human face often helps an organization develop more effective messages and go beyond bombarding an audience with media that only serve to overwhelm it, simply because that audience group has become a group of individuals who live an extremely complex life in which your objective is only one piece of the puzzle at best.

Analyzing a Target Audience: The Art of Asking Questions

Communications objective:
   To educate community leaders and youth in six communities about different ecosystem principles in order to build consensus for possible public policy recommendations.
Target audience #1: local government officials

Possible Questions to Use to Develop a Better Understanding of Members of This Audience

1. Do they recognize environmental problems within their city?

2. Are they involved in local environmental groups?

3. Are they members of donors to national environmental groups?

4. Are they, or is anyone in their families, members of Planet 3000?

5. Has there been any local media coverage of an environmental issue in the last three months?

6. What media do they listen to, watch, read?

7. Who might influence their decision-making process?

8. What experts might influence their decisions about environmental policies?

9. How does the target audience break out in men versus women?

10. How does the target audience break out in age?

11. How does the target audience break out in terms of family (do they have children)?

12. What is the economic outlook in the community?

13. Is there concern about the future quality of life in the community? In the state?

Possible Ways to Gather This Information

1. Look in the American Public Opinion Index to see whether there's been any research done on publics within a 100-mile radius of the community (to find answers to questions 1, 8, and 13).

2. Conduct a media review (all questions).

3. Conduct five in-depth interviews (all questions).

4. Get personal information from public records, media coverage, campaign materials (questions 2–4, 7, and 9–11).

5. Review economic data from government sources on the health of the economy in the community (questions 11 and 12).

6. Check Planet 3000 donor lists. Ask local partner organizations for background information on individual target audience members (questions 2–4).

As these questions are answered, a profile of this audience group will begin to emerge. As other audience groups connected with this objective begin to be analyzed, it is likely that several audiences will have certain things in common. These groups might be "clustered" together when it comes to communicating with them in order to leverage your resources. For example, the same strategies that might be used to reach local government officials might also be used with local business leaders. By clustering groups, you can leverage and maximize the time, money, and effort spent to communicate with them.

Remember: Strategic communications puts the audience first. Everything grows out of that audience-centered focus.

CH0201.DOC

Exercise #4: Identify key audience groups for each of your communications objectives. Where appropriate, include outreach partners. List several characteristics of the different audience groups or, if you don't know something that would be helpful, the questions to ask that would give you insight into the individuals who comprise that audience group. If possible, cluster audience groups by specific characteristics (know which characteristics you're using to cluster the groups).

Next, write a one-paragraph profile of an individual within a given audience group. Remember to give the person a name and describe what he or she looks like in order to give yourself a picture of who it is you want to communicate with.

WORKSHEETS FOR STEP #2

Program Objective #1A

Target audience: _____

Communications Objective #1A

Target audience: _____

Additional audiences: _____

_____   _____

_____   _____

_____   _____

Communications Objective #1B

Target audience: _____

Additional audiences: _____

_____   _____

_____   _____

_____   _____

(Continued)

Communications Objective 1A
Target Audience: _____
Demographic Information

Sex	Occupation
Age range	Race
Income range	Family dwelling location
Education	Family size
Marital status	Life cycle

Geographic Information

Country	City/town/rural/suburb
Region	Neighborhood
State	

Psychographic Information

Activities: work, hobbies, social events, vacations, entertainment, club membership, community activities, shopping, sports

Interests: family, home, job, community, recreation, fashion, food, media, achievements

Opinions: themselves, social issues, politics, business, economic, education, future, culture

- Does this audience have covert power?
- Do its members have power by virtue of their position in the organization or community?
- Are they described by others as knowledgeable or influential on a given issue or in a specific community?
- Are they connected to our organization and why have they chosen to be connected?

Based on the information above, write two or three paragraphs profiling members of this audience. How do they experience life? What drives them? What frightens them? What gives them hope?

Who could help you reach this target audience (outreach partners)? Are these individuals or groups a target audience as well?

_____   ☐ Target   ☐ Not a target

_____   ☐ Target   ☐ Not a target

_____   ☐ Target   ☐ Not a target

_____   ☐ Target   ☐ Not a target

_____   ☐ Target   ☐ Not a target

If any of these individuals or groups are a target audience, do the audience analysis exercise on them so that you know with whom you are communicating.

CHAPTER THREE

Step #3:
What to Say?

Target Your Message

Your organization's messages can be the key to success. While the organization's goals and objectives are the foundation of its communications plan, the message is the heart of its efforts to reach its target audiences. Message development is more art than science, although audience research will help you figure out your target audience's trigger points—what will be influential, what will fall flat, what is likely to conjure up a negative response.

Many of us confuse messages with sound bites, tag lines, slogans, or statements about our organization. While a message may reflect these things—or occasionally incorporate them—it is something much more fundamental and substantive. Indeed, the message is what inspires and anchors sound bites, slogans, and tag lines.

There is no one right way to develop effective messages; everyone does so in the way that works best for them. Because it isn't linear, it is difficult to put the process in chronological order. However, the key steps are as follows:

- Developing key themes
- Deciding on the message frame
- Creating an umbrella message
- Using the message triangle to develop messages

- Examining language and symbols
- Ensuring message discipline

WHAT'S A MESSAGE?

A message should clearly define the issue, connect it to your target audience, and indicate a course of action. A strong message will help your organization achieve its objective—whether that means changing public policy, volunteering to tutor, providing parenting skills to teen mothers, or preventing substance abuse. A message comprises one or two sentences and communicates a complete thought. Three messages—one for Future Generations, one for Planet 3000, and one for the Meridian Health Care Clinic—are provided here as a starting point.

Future Generations:
The next generation should have the opportunity to be born free from chronic health care problems and learning disabilities. By changing public policy, we can guarantee that all women have access to pre-natal care, the key to making this happen. Call 1-800-ACHANCE.

Planet 3000:
In a world spinning out of control, a more balanced life is possible. Natural ecosystems have nurtured life on the planet for millions of years. Join Planet 3000 at Town Hall on October 1st to learn how the laws of nature can enhance your life and your community.

Meridian Health Care Clinic:
People who participate in their own health care live longer, fuller lives. Get smart. Get educated. Call Meridian. It's the only thing standing between you and a better life.

FRAMING AN ISSUE

A strong message defines a problem or an issue in a specific way, delineating the cause of a problem, which in turn will dictate the solution. Some people cast cigarette smoking as a habit that is under the control of an individual—a health problem that only the individual can solve and for which the individual is responsible. Others make the argument that cigarette smoking is a public health problem and should be looked at as the purview of policy makers—when cigarettes are taxed at a higher rate, people (especially teenagers) stop smoking because it is too expensive. A third way to look at the issue is that it is a problem that society must deal with by weeding it out of the popular culture as something attractive or sophisticated. This could be done by convincing businesspeople and artists who control popular culture to alter the portrayal of cigarette smoking.

The first way of defining the problem centers on an individual's role in the problem and the solution, while the second way defines the problem as one that could be addressed by changing public policy and creating systemic change. The third way advocates looking to the private sector for an appropriate response.

Given our country's history of individualism and the tendency to take a more cinematic approach toward what is happening in the world—where news has the feel of storytelling and storytelling has the remnants of tonight's news—it is difficult to expand our view of social problems beyond the limited context of the individual. For some organizations—for example, a literacy group whose volunteers tutor illiterate adults—the way to define the problem may be to address the individuals involved: Learning to read will improve your life by helping you get a better job. Yet the problem might also be looked at as one of limited access to educational resources by certain adult populations. This would require policy makers—or perhaps private business leaders—to find ways to fill the gap by taking steps to reallocate current resources or find new ones. Obviously, how you delineate the problem and the cause of that problem will dictate not only the solution and who's responsible for the solution but how the entire issue is discussed—or *framed*.

Many of society's problems—unemployment, poverty, substance abuse, violence—that are the foci of nonprofit programs can be positioned or debated from either of these frames—as systemic problems in need of a public policy fix or as the problems of individuals who must take responsibility and modify or change their behavior. Sometimes these two frames are in the public's imagination at the same time, vying with each other for primacy and validation. Other times, one frame succeeds for a certain period, only to be overtaken by the other point of view. And while an organization can influence how an issue is framed—especially with key audiences with whom the organization has an existing positive relationship or reputation—there will always be forces beyond the organization's control: other organizations with opposing viewpoints, the economic health of the nation, or the current cultural "lens," which shapes the public consciousness through the news, film, television, music, books, and the like.

Remember: How you frame the problem will dictate what the solution is and how it will be discussed (see Exhibit 3-1).

WHAT'S THE CURRENT FRAME? THE MEDIA REVIEW

To understand how something is currently framed in the public's consciousness—and whether a message is in line with the dominant perspective or whether an organization needs to "reframe" the issue by posing a different, perhaps less pervasive perspective—organizations usually conduct a media review. This doesn't have to be extensive, exhaustive, or expensive, and you don't have to hire an expert to do it—although you will probably want to review your findings with several people within the organization or who are familiar with the issue or program area to reaffirm your interpretation and analysis of the media reviewed.

Exhibit 3-1.   Messages to Frame the Issue

Future Generations

Episodic/personal frame: Women who take advantage of prenatal care become stronger and have healthier babies. You owe it to yourself. Call 1-800-ACHOICE.

Systemic/public policy frame: If all women had access to prenatal care, the state of Pennsylvania could save $50 million dollars in the first two years alone while nurturing a new generation of healthy citizens for Pennsylvania. All it takes is a change in public policy.

Planet 3000

Episodic/personal frame: In a world spinning out of control, a more balanced life is possible. Learn how the laws of nature can change your life.

Systemic/public policy frame: Natural ecosystems have nurtured life on the planet for millions of years. Yet we are destroying our planet, one law at a time, the wrong law at the wrong time. Turn it around. The right law at the right time.

Meridian

Episodic/personal frame: People who participate in their own healthcare can improve the quality of their lives. Take action to get healthy. Get educated. It's the only thing standing between you and a better life.

Systemic/public policy frame: People who have a chance to participate in their health care can improve the quality of their lives. Ensure that everyone has that chance through a national health insurance program.

Select several media outlets that influence your audiences. In some instances, you may want to include local and national news media, both broadcast and print, as well as infotainment or entertainment programs that may have a particularly high impact on your target audiences and/or in your community: talk shows, while not necessarily "news," can have a strong influence on public opinion to which policy makers respond.

Once you have identified the outlets and programs to monitor, review the coverage of your issue, program, or concern for a specific amount of time—for example, a random week or two. You want enough sources to provide a broad view of the issue or concern, yet not so many as to overwhelm you and/or whoever is working on the task at hand. Organize the clips by outlet, by date, or both to spot trends as you go along. You may want to use discrete mentions in order to assess the range of attitudes toward the issue or portrayals of individuals for whom the issue is a problem. For example, there may be an article on homelessness that mentions a variety of individuals— single mothers, children, the unemployed, people with AIDS. If you are studying the coverage of a population—that is, single mothers—this story would be part of your review in order for you to see how single mothers are portrayed (in a story not specifically about single mothers). If, on the other hand, you are looking at the problem of homelessness—as opposed to at a single population—you would want to analyze how the causes of the problem are defined and who is being called on to respond to the problem.

As you review the coverage, use the following types of questions to get your media review started. It might be useful to create a matrix or a grid to help you analyze the data once the coverage has been reviewed.

Guiding Questions

- How is the problem defined?
- What solutions, if any, are given?
- Who is identified as responsible for creating the problem?
- Who is held accountable for solving the problem?
- Is the problem portrayed as the plight of the individual or the problem of a larger group? Of society in general?
- Is there a connection between the individual and the environment in which that individual lives/experiences the problem? (For example, if it is a story about the plight of a homeless family, is there a discussion of the amount of low-income housing available or unavailable? Is there any link between homelessness and current economic indicators as compared to other times in the country's history?)

- What isn't being said? What is being left out and thereby marginalized or portrayed as less legitimate?
- What is the emotional subtext of the coverage?
- What images (if any) are used to illustrate the story?
- What and whose opinions are featured and deemed valid or important?

As you do this type of analysis, it is likely that patterns will begin to emerge. If the predominant frame is complementary to your organization's position, you have a strong foundation on which to build momentum. On the other hand, if the coverage doesn't depict a problem, concern, or issue in a way that reflects your organization's position, values, or understanding of the problem, you will need to pick apart the current positioning—or *framework.* Look at the assumptions, arguments, or rationales. What needs to be highlighted or explained to move the issue in a new direction? What information and/or emotional context is needed to shift the public's perception of the problem and its causes?

The Berkeley Media Studies Group, a public health media advocacy organization that specializes in framing analysis, looked in September 1995 at how children and youth were framed in U.S. newspapers in an effort to help children's organizations get a realistic picture of how children, youth, and issues related to them were being defined by the press to the public—in this case, policy makers and influentials who read newspapers. The researchers reported that children and youth, when portrayed in the context of discrete news incidents, almost always appeared as victims. In articles about "adult" or public policy issues, children's innocence and vulnerability were highlighted, often to instill moral outrage or intensify a call to action. Yet, when teens or youth were cited as examples in these articles, it was always in a negative light.[1]

Although the researchers drew a number of conclusions, perhaps the most disturbing for organizations working to improve the lives of children in this country was that the findings suggested that such organizations "face a particular challenge in moving children's issues into the news—and into the minds of policy makers—in a substantive way. Children are used to raise sympathy for issues that have relatively little to do with them, while those programs that in fact are very relevant to their lives, such as Medicaid, remain defined firmly as adult issues."[2] The key here is to remember that the primary audience of advocates is policy makers and policy makers are influenced by

---

[1] Berkeley Media Studies Group, *Frames on Children and Youth in U.S. Newspapers,* September 1995.
[2] Berkeley Media Studies Group, p. 15.

newspapers—with some newspapers having more influence than others. This portrayal of children and youth—a frame within which children and youth are consistently viewed—makes it more difficult for policy makers to see children and youth in an honest and real way. This, of course, translates into a lack of appropriate and intelligent public policy to deal with the many problems that children in our society face day after day, year after year.

This type of media review and analysis will provide you with valuable strategic information that you can use to develop more effective messages because (1) you will be able to incorporate, co-opt, or respond to current assumptions and arguments with your messages and (2) you will understand how the various pieces of the current frame fit together, which will enable you to pull apart the pieces and reconstruct a new frame. This repositioning of an issue is often called *reframing the debate.*

FOUR KEY THEMES

Every organization needs more than a single message for an issue or program. Ideally, your organization should have three or four key themes that help you formulate messages that anyone from within the organization can use to talk about the issue with others. These themes provide the emotional grist that best responds to challenges, arguments, or questions that may arise while resonating most readily with a number of populations. The themes can then be "mixed and matched," creating messages that reinforce each other as well as reinforcing how your organization is defining the problem and the solution.

For example, a goal of the organization Future Generations is to guarantee prenatal care for low-income women throughout the state of Pennsylvania. First, we look for the larger themes or arguments that will resonate with (in this case) policy makers and voters. It is around these themes that the organization will create key messages (see Exhibit 3-2) using the message triangle:

- *Fewer chronic health care problems:* When expectant mothers receive prenatal care, there is a dramatic drop in the rate of chronic health care problems in their children.

- *Healthy mothers:* Expectant mothers who learn how to take care of themselves during pregnancy continue to do so afterward.

- *Fewer learning disabilities:* When expectant mothers receive prenatal care, their children are less likely to have learning disabilities.

- *Government saves money:* Less is spent on health care and education.

Exhibit 3-2.   Future Generations Themes

Government saves money

<table>
<tr>
<td>Fewer learning disabilities
in the next generation</td>
<td>**Objective:**
Guarantee
prenatal care,
change public policy</td>
<td>Healthy mothers</td>
</tr>
</table>

Fewer chronic health care problems

What this does is give the organization several ways to respond to the issue, all of which reinforce the objective of guaranteeing prenatal care for low-income women. Imagine a policy maker or reporter asking why legislation should be passed to guarantee prenatal care. Using these themes, the spokesperson might reply in a variety of ways. To illustrate this, three examples are provided.

> "The next generation should have the opportunity to be born free from chronic health care problems and learning disabilities. By changing public policy, we can guarantee that all women have access to prenatal care, the key to making this happen."

> "If all women had access to prenatal care, the state of Pennsylvania could save 50 million dollars[3] in the first two years alone while nurturing a new generation of healthy citizens for Pennsylvania. All it takes is a change in public policy."

> "Women who have prenatal care not only become healthier during their pregnancy, but they remain healthier and give birth to healthier babies. By changing public policy and guaranteeing all women access to prenatal care, we can nurture not just one but two generations of healthy citizens for the state of Pennsylvania."

The key to doing this, of course, is to always come back to your objective so that, no matter what the positioning of the issue, it is repeated again and again—to change public policy. When this is done, there's a better chance that the message will actually break through the clutter into the target audience's consciousness.

---

[3] This is an example only and is not based on research. It is assumed that the organization would have access to actual research data, know what the true dollar amount would be, and be able to use it in the message.

THE UMBRELLA MESSAGE:
WHY IT'S IMPORTANT TO SOCIETY

This is the universal message—the one that defines the organization and clarifies its mission (see Exhibit 3-3). It has three components. *What it is* defines the organization; *what it means* is why the organization and/or its mission is important to society or the community; *what to do* is what your organization would like to see society or the community do to support the mission. This message encompasses the values and the positions of the organization, which is why it is called an umbrella message. Inasmuch as possible, symbolic language should be used in an umbrella message to capture the attention of both emotional and more rational audience members.

DEVELOPING EFFECTIVE MESSAGES:
THE MESSAGE TRIANGLE

Three elements make up any effective message.

1. *What it is:* An explanation of the problem, the program, the issue, the service. Usually this element remains constant throughout and is influenced primarily by your organization's values, knowledge, and experience. It is the common thread that runs through all your messages with respect to this objective, no matter which audience your organization is addressing. It is this aspect of the message that most effectively frames an issue—e.g., the problem and its cause.

Exhibit 3-3   Developing Effective Messages: The Message Triangle

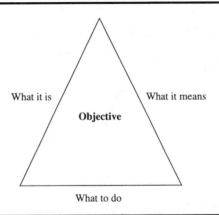

2. *What it means:* This will tell an audience why this issue, problem, program, or service is important to it—often expressed in marketing circles as "what's in it for me?" Usually it is this element of the message that gives us the effective lead when addressing a specific target audience, because it goes to the heart of audience members' concerns. Ideally, you want to be able to tailor this in response to different target audiences. Why should an individual pay attention, be concerned, take action? Interestingly, this aspect of the message also can be used to segment audiences.

3. *What to do:* This component is often the same for several audience groups. Sometimes it may be phrased as a more subtle "request"—such as asking someone to look at something differently. Obviously, the effectiveness of this type of message may be more difficult to measure. For example, public opinion may shift on an issue over many months but may not result in any concrete action taken or not taken by individuals, policy makers, or other stakeholders. Indeed, this element of the message equation may change over time as the political, social, or economic landscape changes.

Most often the message is geared to the action component of your communications plan—call for more information, ask your local PTA, vote YES on Referendum 21, change your diet, and so on. It must be positive, persuasive, and possible. Each of the examples uses the message triangle to organize the message:

Future Generations

What it is	By changing public policy, we can guarantee that all women have access to prenatal care.
What it means	The next generation should have the opportunity to be born free from chronic health care problems and learning disabilities.
What to do	The key to making this happen: Call 1-800-ACHOICE.

Planet 3000

What it is	Natural ecosystems have nurtured life on the planet for millions of years.

What it means   In a world spinning out of control, a more balanced life is possible.

What to do   Join Planet 3000 at Town Hall on October 1st to learn how the laws of nature can enhance your life and your community.

Meridian Health Care Clinic

What it is   People who participate in their own health care live longer, fuller lives.

What it means   It's the only thing standing between you and a better life.

What to do   Get smart. Get educated. Call Meridian.

WHO DETERMINES THE MESSAGE

The essence of a message is based on how the people involved in an organization think and feel about the issue, their program, or a concern, as well as how you wish the solution to be discussed. The most successful messages are expressed in ways that resonate with the perspective, experience, and values of the target audience. (Remember that this often is not the same as *your* perceptions of a target audience's values, opinions, attitudes, or beliefs. Effective messages speak to an audience's actual experience of the world in which they live. This is why audience research, described in Chapter 2, is so critical. Also see Chapter 7 for using focus groups to evaluate your message development effort.)

Good messages balance your organization's values, goals, and objectives with the beliefs, attitudes, and opinions of your target audiences. And, if the problem and the solution are defined within the framework of your audience's perspective and values, it is much more likely that the audience will at least listen to your message and agree with how you've framed the issue—the first step in getting someone to think about and possibly agree with the solution you're suggesting.

Unless your organization has a very close and positive relationship to a specific audience—for example, your organization has so much clout with members from a target audience that, on hearing or seeing that the message comes from you, they will be motivated to act—or the objective is directly related to attracting clients, activists, donors, and so on to the organization, featuring the name of your organization prominently in your message may not be necessary or advantageous.

For example, the Planet 3000 message speaks to the feeling of many people that "life is spinning out of control" and uses this as a way to build rapport with the target audience. The solution for many people would be to create "balance" in their lives. This is tied to the values of Planet 3000 in its effort to get individuals to apply the laws of nature to create balance in their lives and in the community. While the audience would agree with the organization's perspective on the problem, it might not agree with the solution; but the organization, in creating the message in a way that resonates with the audience's own experience, is one step closer to moving the audience toward the proposed solution.

MATCHING THE MESSAGE TO THE AUDIENCE

Often what you want individuals to do about the problem, issue, or concern and why they should pay attention changes from audience to audience. For example, if you were targeting young pregnant women for prenatal services, you would want them to call your organization for prenatal care. If you were targeting a policy maker to provide additional funding to support prenatal care services, you might want him or her to cosponsor legislation. So, while the subject—the need for prenatal care services—remains the same, why the subject is important to the two audiences changes, as well as what you want the audiences to do about it. (Note, however, that the two messages do not in any way contradict each other. Indeed, they could arguably be stitched into a seamless message with one supporting the other.)

Obviously, the key aspect of a message addresses your audience's most direct concern. If you did your homework, what it means to the audience will resonate on an emotional as well as a rational level. So, while the reasoning will be based on truth and facts, the context and language should be emotionally charged.

A final point to remember is that audiences are people first and audiences second. Because of this, their interpretation of the message goes beyond receiving it in a vacuum. First, there are other messages—some that are in conflict, others that have nothing to do with your message but are part of the communications environment vying for attention. These messages may be one-way or they may be delivered as part of an ongoing dialogue between the recipient and other people who may or may not be connected to the organization. This ongoing *negotiation* of the message by audience members is key to understanding the effects of communications programs. It is a much more useful paradigm than one of domination—"if we can dominate the airwaves, we'll succeed"—or of persuasion, the two most common approaches to communications by organizations.[4]

LANGUAGE: SIMPLE, SYMBOLIC, AND EMOTIONAL

It is important that messages be truthful as well as clear, persuasive, and concise. The language we use conveys more than the simple meaning of the words. Language suggests the images that will be used to convey our messages. Some words trigger an emotional response, while others convey the need for a more rational approach. Note that some words may bring about a positive feeling in some audiences while at the same time conjuring up negative or uncomfortable emotions in others. For example, "variety" may be a welcome thing to some people because it implies choice, while to others it may create uncertainty—for example, "just tell me what to do." "Change" may convey excitement and new opportunities for some, but it can just as easily raise the specter of anxiety and fear of the unknown in others. Know how your audience will interpret or respond to words that carry dual meanings.

Get rid of words that have been overused or that have no emotional punch, words that we have come to rely on too much. Some favorites that make a lot of organizations' lists are:

- Services
- Programs
- Unique
- Innovative
- Facilitate
- Comprehensive

Never underestimate the power of symbolic language to convey the emotional context and the values that we want to have connected to our messages and our missions. Symbols have been used by storytellers for centuries

---

[4] The notion of negotiating messages was first conceptualized by E. Katz in "Communications Research Since Lazarsfeld," *Public Opinion Quarterly*, 51(4), 1987, p. S38 as cited in Dozier and Ehling, p. 165.

and can often conjure up conscious as well as unconscious emotions or responses. By connecting the right symbols and values to your cause, issue, or concern and associating them truthfully with your objectives, you can not only solidify existing support but also win converts to your position. Some popular symbols and/or values used by different organizations, movements, or commercial companies follow. All of these words could easily have one or several images attached to them to heighten their symbolic meaning as well.

Freedom	Oppression
Privacy	Deceit
Equality	Greed
Individualism	Dependency
Fairness	Favoritism
Security	Suspicion
Family	Fraud
Opportunity	Problem
Honesty	

One of the biggest challenges when developing messages is the tendency to use jargon or terms common to a given field. These terms mean something obvious to those working in that field, but to everyone else, the words aren't readily understood and lack resonance (they are not common to the audience member's life experience). For example:

Jargon	Plain English
Intervention	Help, counsel
Facilitate	Bring together
Assessment	Study

Another language consideration when creating messages is the four social styles that influence how individuals respond to information and create opinions—Analytical, Driver, Amiable, and Expressive (see Exhibit 3-4). Two elements combine to create these styles that have to do with processing information and communication:

1. Does the person process information analytically or intuitively?

2. Does the person tend to be more assertive or less assertive?

Exhibit 3-4. The Four Social Styles

Analytical	*Driver*
Tends to be cautious	Competitive and independent
Likes controlled environment	Tends to dominate
Agreeable, serious, persistent	Wants immediate results
Likes status quo, follows the rules	Very decisive, wants direct answers
Diplomatic, obliging	Adventurous, persistent, outspoken
Checks accuracy, very orderly	Tends to cause action
Amiable	*Expressive*
Dislikes conflict	Tends to generate enthusiasm
Tends to be thorough, patient	Very confident, likes change
Takes time to listen	Likes working with people
Has demonstrated loyalty	Often very optimistic
Wants agreement	Has desire to help others
Likes security/status quo	Tends to be persuasive

It is unusual for someone to be completely one way or another. Usually people fall somewhere in between. However, if someone processed information primarily from an analytical perspective but also had an emotional side, those emotional qualities would color the analytical tendency in ways more characteristic of the Amiable person and not the Expressive person.

- *Analytical:* Some people will be swayed more by rational or logical arguments that they can analyze with little emotion, primarily alone since they tend to be more passive in their approach than assertive or outgoing. Economic data, social indicators, and research findings tend to convince this group most effectively.

- *Amiable:* These people are highly emotive in their approach to life, and an emotional message will work best with them. They also tend to be more introverted or passive than assertive in how they function in the world, so that radical approaches would tend to make them uncomfortable.

- *Driver:* This type of person also prefers a message based on logic, facts, research, and statistics, but framed in a more emotional way than would appeal to his or her counterpart, the Analytical person.

- *Expressive:* This type of person is also assertive but is more comfortable with emotional messages and prefers intuitive reasoning, like his or her counterpart, the Amiable person.

Think about the language that would resonate with each of these four social styles, the framing and call to action that they would respond to. In some instances, different parts of a single message may resonate with individuals from each of the four social styles. In any message, the themes will attract people's attention and the language will color the meaning of the message for individuals from each of these four social styles (see Exhibit 3-5).

Finally, go through your messages once more and see whether you can simplify the language so that your audience understands exactly what you are saying without your having to explain what you mean. Ideally, someone with an eighth-grade reading level should be able to understand what you're talking about and what you mean.

TESTING MESSAGES

When messages reach the marketplace of ideas, they take on a life of their own. People attach their own experiences, emotions, and opinions to the original message and believe that this revised version is the "real" or "origi-

Exhibit 3-5   Achieving Objectives through the Four Social Styles

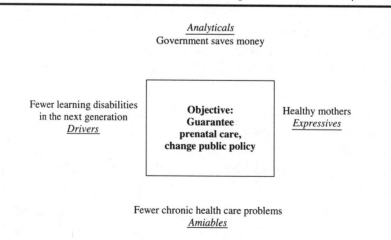

Analyticals
Government saves money

Fewer learning disabilities
in the next generation
Drivers

**Objective:
Guarantee
prenatal care,
change public policy**

Healthy mothers
Expressives

Fewer chronic health care problems
Amiables

nal" message. The upside to this is that your message has become the "prop-erty" of others and has taken root in your audience's consciousness, getting passed along from one person to another, from one medium to another. The downside is that while it is human nature for people to color any message or information with their own attitudes, cultural norms, stereotypes, or expec-tations, these shadings can alter the original message considerably, perhaps making it more foe than friend! This "assimilation" of the message, in fact, is one of the prime reasons messages are co-opted in order to destabilize and disrupt their momentum in the marketplace of ideas. Often, this is done through language and symbols, which is why it is so important to test the strength and durability of the messages you've developed. Commercial companies often contribute money to preserving a national monument in exchange for the chance to cloak themselves in that symbol of freedom and new beginnings. This was done by many corporations and organizations during the restoration of the Statue of Liberty leading up to the bicentennial celebration in 1976.

Ideally, you want to bring together a few individuals who represent your different target audiences and see which messages—or elements of those messages—resonate with which audiences. Focus groups conducted by a professional with experience in teasing out the nuances of various messages can prove invaluable, but they also can be expensive. If you have limited resources and have to test your messages yourself, make sure that whoever is leading the discussion is good at putting people at ease. You should also have a few key staff members (or volunteers) observing the groups' reactions. If possible, videotape—or at least audiotape—what is said in order to capture the language used by the group. Here are some things to consider when test-ing your messages:

- Are the groups responding emotionally to the language you've cho-sen? If yes, is it everyone or just representatives from one audience group?
- Do they perceive "what it is" as true and legitimate?
- Do they agree with "why it's important" enough to take the action? If yes, what is it that most convinced them? If no, what might make them see the message as important?
- Do they agree with the logic you're presenting? How quickly did they come to agree with it?
- Are they confused by any assumptions you've made? By the language you've used?

- How do they translate the message immediately after elements are presented versus after it's been discussed?

- What did you learn about how they perceive the problem and why they hold those opinions?

- Did anyone eventually "take ownership" of any of the messages—or elements of the messages—for example, did people say these back to the group in their own words? What was their attitude and body language when they did so?

This type of exercise, no matter how unscientific, is valuable if for no other reason than that (1) you've tested your messages and found out where the weak spots are and (2) you've met people who are actually representative of your target audiences whom you can now hold in your mind's eye as you continue to reach out to those audience groups.

MESSAGE DISCIPLINE

Once you've decided on your strongest messages, you need to make sure that all those affiliated with the organization know what the messages are, can say them in their own words if necessary, and understand the importance of sticking to those messages when the issue, program, or concern is discussed or written about. This can be done by circulating the messages—and a few talking points for each message that help flesh out the message—on a regular basis with a reminder to staff, board, and volunteers that these messages should guide how they present the matter. In addition, any media your organization produces—newsletters, brochures, videotapes, Web sites, and so on—should repeat and reinforce these messages.

While you and your colleagues may get tired of the same message, don't assume that your audience has assimilated it. According to marketing guru Jay Levinson, a message needs to be received twenty-seven times before it actually registers with the recipient. Indeed, commercial companies spend millions of dollars to reinforce slogans and jingles that are heard and seen again and again, and only after much exposure does the individual remember the words and attribution. So much more so for messages dealing with complex social issues! Once you've come this far, you owe it to your organization, to your mission, and to your stakeholders to use message discipline to enforce "staying on message" by everyone connected to your organization.

Exercise #5

a) Decide how you want to frame your issue. Will you use existing frames, use part of those frames, or attempt to move the existing frame toward a new frame?

b) Choose three or four themes that you will develop in your messages that will resonate with your target audiences.

c) Create an umbrella message for your objective or organization.

d) Create at least one target message, using the message triangle, for each of your target audiences. Remember that one or two parts of the message may stay the same and that the part that may need to be altered is the explanation of why it is important to that audience.

e) Examine closely each word you've used in your target messages. Is it jargon-free? Is it emotional? Clear? Concise? Persuasive?

f) Provide staff and board members with clean copies of the message, indicating the target audience to get their feedback. Incorporate as appropriate.

g) Test the messages more broadly with members of the target audience(s) (usually via focus groups), and incorporate the feedback as appropriate. Distribute clean copies of the "final" messages to staff, board, and volunteers, explaining the importance of "staying on message" when they discuss the issue with friends, family, clients, activists, or strangers.

WORKSHEETS FOR STEP #3

Goal #1

Objective #1A

Current Message Frame
How is the problem/solution being discussed? What words are used to describe the problem, people who are affected by the problem, people working on the solution? Who or what is controlling or dictating the frame?

Desired Message Frame
How do we want the problem/solution discussed? What words could help us better describe the problem, people who are affected by the problem, people working on the solution so as to reframe the issue?

Key Themes

```
┌─────────────────────────────────┐
│  Objective:                     │
│                                 │
│                                 │
│                                 │
│                                 │
│                                 │
└─────────────────────────────────┘
```

Umbrella Message

Target audience:_____

What it is   **What it means**

_____   _____

_____   _____

_____   _____

_____   _____

What should the audience do about it?

_____

(Continued)

Message for target audience:_____

Language check

- ❑ Clear
- ❑ Persuasive
- ❑ Emotional
- ❑ Concise
- ❑ Good use of symbols
- ❑ What images does this message convey?
- ❑ What values does this message convey?
- ❑ Are they in line with our organization's values?
- ❑ Are they in line with our audience's values?
- ❑ Did we use jargon?

- ❑ Could my 14-year-old nephew or niece understand this message?
- ❑ Will the audience perceive "what it is" as true and legitimate?
- ❑ Will they agree with "what it means to them"?
- ❑ Is the action asked of the audience doable?

Step #4:
How to Communicate It?

Practical Strategies, Appropriate Vehicles

The next step is to figure out how best to communicate with various target audiences over time in order to achieve your communications objective—to make them aware of an issue, to move them to take an action, to change their thinking or attitude toward an issue or to develop a closer relationship with your organization and its mission. This is a three-part process. First, you must decide on the strategies that are most appropriate to your audiences and objectives; second, you must figure out which vehicles are needed to make each strategy happen; and third, you must assess which vehicles and strategies overlap (serve several audiences simultaneously), so that you can maximize limited resources.

WHY CHOOSE ONE STRATEGY
OR VEHICLE OVER ANOTHER?

Every strategy—and every vehicle used to facilitate a strategy—has unique attributes that make it attractive to different audiences at different times. Obviously, what may be a positive strategy at a certain time with a given audience may have a negative effect with that same audience at a different time. A simple example is a phone call. At work, people expect phone calls from people they don't know—new vendors, potential clients or volunteers, and so forth—but the same people might not appreciate phone calls from strangers—telemarketing companies, political campaigns asking for money, market researchers, and so on—while they are at home.

To help decide on the appropriateness of different strategies with different audiences, seven criteria can be used. In different situations, some criteria will be more important to consider than others. Yet they are all factors in the eventual success of any communications strategy your organization decides to implement.

1. Audience responsiveness

2. The organization's relationship to the audience

3. How the strategy or vehicle will influence the audience's perception

4. Who controls the message

5. Effort to implement

6. Budget issues

7. Potential use with other audiences

Lists of specific vehicles as well as factual information and "rules of the road" for each category are provided in the Appendixes to stimulate your thinking as to how you might reach the audiences you've targeted. These lists are not meant to be exhaustive. Rather, they are given to help you brainstorm options to consider and aid you in your decision-making process.

THE SEVEN CRITERIA

Audience Responsiveness

While this first point may seem obvious in light of earlier chapters, your audience's day-to-day routines and experience of the world will determine how receptive it will be to a given strategy or vehicle. It is within these parameters—someone's day-to-day life—that your organization will communicate with the audience. Some things to consider when deciding on the appropriateness of different strategies and vehicles for target audiences are outlined below.

Guiding Questions

- At what point in the day are they likely to be most receptive to your approach (when will your message be welcomed as opposed to being perceived as an intrusion or extraneous)?
- What vehicles are they likely to encounter?
- Of those, which ones will they stop and notice?
- Of those, which are they likely to spend time with?
- Of those, which are likely to influence them; which are they likely to look at more than once; which are they likely to share with others?

The Organization's Relationship to the Audience and/or the Messenger

Often, a specific strategy will only be effective if your organization has a relationship—or, at the very least, an understanding—with an audience member. For example, an unsolicited fax sent to someone who has not asked to be on a notification list or who has never before responded to your organization is likely to be disregarded by the recipient because a fax is still considered to be a communication that requires an agreed-upon relationship. On the other hand, receiving a letter in the mail from an organization or a phone call from a complete stranger has become more acceptable in modern society.

When an organization relies on an "outreach partner" or third-party messenger—such as the press or another organization—it not only must consider its relationship to that third-party messenger (which, in and of itself, constitutes an audience), but must also look at the relationship of that messenger to the primary target audience. For example, the relationship between the daily newspaper and your target audience (do they read the daily newspaper?) will be just as important to consider as your organization's relationship to reporters and editors at the daily newspaper. Obviously, if your organization doesn't have a relationship with someone at the paper, it will be more difficult to count on that messenger to deliver your message in part or as a whole.

CH0401.DOC

Exercise #6: Picture your organization at the heart of a concentric circle, where you and your staff are at the innermost circle because you are the core group of individuals who have a daily, proactive commitment to making the organization work and to seeing that the organization's mission is advanced. (See Exhibit 4-1 for the Planet 3000 concentric circles model.)

Exhibit 4-1   Planet 3000 Audience Groups

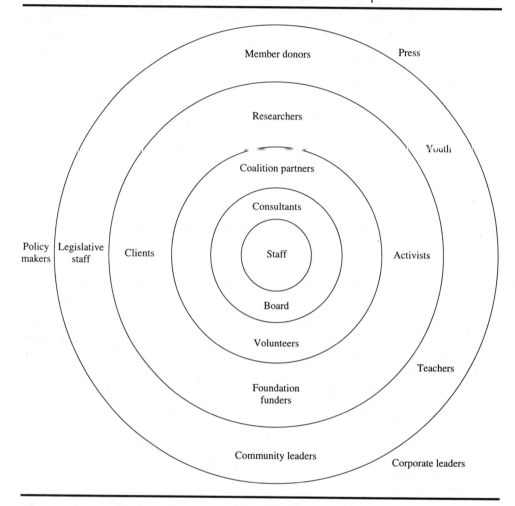

Include the following audience groups on the circle: staff, board, activists, volunteers, clients, consultants/advisors, press, community leaders, funders, corporate leaders, policy makers, and so on.

Some issues to help guide this process might include:

- What is the relationship of this audience to our organization? (On a scale of 1 to 10, how closely allied with our organization do individual audience members feel?)

- Has our organization communicated with this person/ audience before?

- If yes, how? What was the response (if any)?
- If yes, how frequently do we communicate with this individual or audience?
- Have we ever engaged in interactive communication with this individual or audience? (If yes, it is more likely the audience member will see him- or herself as having a connection to your organization.)

Now, working your way out, place your organization's target audiences at an appropriate distance from the heart of the organization yet somewhere within the concentric circle. Obviously, the closer an audience group is to the heart of the circle, the easier it will be to catch that audience's attention and communicate with it in the manner that is most conducive to the business at hand. The further away from the core of the organization you get, the more limited are your choices of vehicles and/or the more careful you must be in selecting which vehicle to use and when to use it.

One way to begin to make sense of why some vehicles are more appropriate than others for specific audiences is to consider your own preferences in different circumstances.

1. How do you like to receive information
   - At home?
   - At work?
   - While travelling?

2. How do you like to communicate or interact with one other person
   - Socially?
   - For business?

3. How do you prefer communicating with a group of people
   - Socially?
   - For work?
   - For learning?

4. How do you like to learn about something new?
   - Books
   - Classroom or seminar
   - Online

5. How do you prefer learning more about a subject you already know something about?

- Books
- Magazines, periodicals
- Meetings
- Online

Influence on Perceptions

Perceptions are at the heart of our opinions, beliefs, and value systems. They are a mix of rational thought about and emotional experience of the world. Different strategies tip the scales one way or another, and your objective will dictate whether it is better to take a more emotional approach or to use a strategy that speaks to the more rational side of a person's experience. Indeed, how other organizations portray the issue as well as the social and political environments that create the backdrop for an individual's perceptions also must be considered when weighing the potential impact of different strategies.

Consider how you might perceive a housing crisis. A newspaper article provides a wealth of details, perhaps a picture or two, and you get an in-depth understanding of the crisis. Now, imagine that same subject covered on the six o'clock news—perhaps a ninety-second story with clips of homeless people huddled together against the cold and policy makers debating legislation followed by a clip of the mayor climbing out of a limousine and offering views on the matter. The juxtaposition of these "live" visual images will have a very different impact on your perception of the problem and the solutions. A final treatment might be in the form of a town meeting conducted by your organization that brings together not only the people most affected but also those who have the ability to do something about the problem. You audiotape the meeting and send out edited versions to possible supporters with a direct mail piece. This third option will cause yet another type of understanding to take hold within the audience it is intended to reach—it probably generates a less emotional reaction than the video treatment but very possibly a more emotional response than the print story (see Exhibit 4-2).

Another thing to consider when using a third party to deliver your message is how that party's role or status in the community may color the target audience's perception. The press validates and lends weight to issues that it covers, with most people perceiving a certain objectivity in the facts presented. If individuals within your target audience are members of another organiza-

Exhibit 4-2   Vehicles Carry the Message

Communications vehicles are the methods or media you use to carry your message to your different audiences. Vehicles—whether your organization or a third party produces them—can be segmented into different categories.

	Traditional	*Mass media*	*New technology*
Print	Newsletters	Magazines	Fax on demand
Face-to-face	Meetings	Press briefings	Groupware
Audio only	Phone calls	Radio	Auditorium teleconferencing
Audio and video	Videotapes	Television	Videoconferencing
Computer-facilitated	Word processing	Wire services	Internet/CD-ROM

tion, they may respond more readily to the message when it is delivered by that organization than they would if it were delivered by your organization, with which they have no relationship. The reputation of the messenger influences the reception and perception of the message. Some issues to consider when deciding which strategies and vehicles will be the most effective are outlined below.

Guiding Questions

- Will this particular audience be moved by a more rational approach to the issue or a more emotional telling of the story?

- In the past, has this topic or issue been framed primarily in a rational way, an emotional way, or a combination of the two?

- How would a certain type of documentation—a videotape of factory emissions versus an audio storytelling versus a print fact sheet—tell the same story differently?

- Does this audience need help visualizing the problem?

- Does this audience need an in-depth understanding of the facts that are causing this problem?

- Does this audience need help thinking through possible solutions to the problem?

- Does this audience need a more direct experience of the problem—that is, does it need to interact with staff, clients, and so forth to feel more connected to the problem?

Who Controls the Message

There are two elements to who controls the message, no matter what strategy is used to deliver it: the producer of the vehicle and the recipient of it. The producer can be the organization, someone the organization hires, or a third party with no connection to the organization—for example, the press. As the producer role moves further and further away from the organization's control, so too does the guarantee that the message will accurately reflect the organization's perspective. For example, an organization with an in-house editorial staff may produce reports, Web site information, and op-eds that can become the voice of the organization.

When a freelance writer or video producer is hired, staff can brief that person about the issue and give him or her background materials and people to talk to, but in the end the freelance writer will write in a different voice— perhaps saying what the organization wants to say, but not in the same way as the in-house editorial staff. That same material can be presented to a reporter at an interview or a press briefing, and the end result is usually a mix of your organization's message and facts it presented, other messages, other facts, and a retelling that may or may not reflect your message accurately. And, no matter how accurate or sympathetic the article may be, it will certainly not reflect the voice of the organization.

The second half of message control is even more elusive because the recipients—readers, viewers, listeners, users, participants—will interpret the message that is delivered based on their own experiences, prejudices, opinions, attitudes, values, and beliefs, over which an organization has virtually no control. The most we can do is research our target audience as much as possible and aim our vehicles like a laser beam at that audience group so that our message comes close to being interpreted as we meant it to be interpreted. Some questions to consider when deciding on the appropriateness of different strategies and vehicles for target audiences are provided in the following list.

Guiding Questions

- How important is it to control the message/set of facts presented (what is left out as well as what is included)?

- How important is it to tell the story broadly versus telling it accurately (from our organization's point of view)?

- What can we do to help ensure an accurate interpretation of our message by the target audience (possible feedback mechanisms, interactive follow-up opportunities)?

- What vehicles does our organization currently produce that clearly reflect the voice of the organization?

- Do these vehicles tend to be in one medium more than other media—that is, more print than audio, more electronic than video?

- If so, why is this? (Audience? Comfort level of staff in one medium? Complexity of message?)

Effort to Implement

This is all about the time and level of expertise available to your organization that will be required to make something happen. Part of the communications decision-making process must take into account the complexity of the tasks that will need to be done to actualize the various strategies in the plan, the amount of time it will take to achieve each piece that makes up the total strategy or vehicle, and whose time will be taken up in this process. Furthermore, it is not simply that one strategy needs to be considered; rather, the entire plan needs to be looked at as a whole. Strategies may be delayed because, while the results would be well worth the time and effort expended, there are too many other things to do during the month for which the strategy was originally planned. If that's the case, will the strategy be just as valid and effective later in the year as it would have been had it happened at the planned time?

Frequently, organizations commit to a complex strategy—or even something "simple" like a monthly newsletter—without figuring out how much staff time it will take to accomplish all the tasks involved. The result is unrealistic—and often unmet—deadlines. How can an organization judge whether the effort is worth the expected impact? Aside from asking others who may have done something similar, some issues to consider when determining whether a strategy is worth the time and effort are outlined in the following list.

Guiding Questions

- How much lead time do you have or need before the vehicle will be used?

- How much time will it take staff to produce this vehicle?

- Will each staff member involved work exclusively on this project? If not, how will members' other work impact these deadlines?

- Will we need to bring in outside help to meet the deadline?

- If a consultant will be used or the press will be approached to package the message, how much time will it take for staff to initiate the process, follow up, and work with these outside individuals to ensure that the message delivered is as close as possible to that desired?

Budget Issues

A strategy is only appropriate if it is affordable. One aspect of this—staff and consulting time—is discussed in the preceding text. If those costs can be covered and the time demands can be met, the next consideration will be "out-of-pocket" costs, such as printing, graphic design, postage, telephone charges, room rentals, travel, speakers' fees, refreshments, and so on. At this stage it is less important to tally a detailed budget than it is to estimate the range for these expenses and, given that range, whether the strategies are truly an option for your organization.

While there is no magic formula for a communications budget, most successful nonprofits—both large and small—work with communications budgets that are 8 to 12 percent of their total organizational budgets, with many advocacy groups exceeding even the high end of that range. Unfortunately, most organizations don't recognize their total spending on communications functions and, as a result, don't allow themselves room to reallocate costs from one type of strategy to another type that has proven to be more effective. For example, instead of doing a first-class mailing of a one-page memo or letter to 300 people, you could decide to do a broadcast fax instead. Thus, the postage and printing budget for that mailing—approximately $195—would be reallocated to your telecommunications charges of approximately $120. (In this case, there would be a savings as well as a reallocation.) Some questions to consider when deciding on the affordability of different strategies and vehicles for target audiences are provided in the following list.

Guiding Questions

- Is the cost of this strategy realistic for the size of our organization's budget?
- Is there a way to reallocate existing resources to realize a "bigger bang for the buck"?
- Can we raise the money needed for this strategy or vehicle? (How much time would it take to secure that type of contribution? Do we have it? Is that time well spent?)

- Are there ways we could defray the cost through in-kind contributions? (How much time would it take to secure that type of contribution? Do we have it? Is that time well spent?)

Potential Use with Other Audiences

Just as different strategies can have an impact on other audiences, so too can vehicles be produced and used with multiple audiences. While this is done more often than not, nonprofits need to become more aware that broadcasting materials to multiple audiences without tailoring them may backfire. Given the amount of information pouring into people's lives at home, at work, even at social gatherings, it will be increasingly difficult for a single vehicle—whether a newsletter, video, audioconference, Web page, or annual meeting—to address a variety of audiences, because fewer and fewer individuals want to hunt for the one or two things that are of interest to them within the "consumate vehicle," especially if the items of interest aren't the first things they see.

A good example of how commercial enterprises are dealing with this phenomenon is major national magazines that put different covers on the same issue in order to attract different audiences. While a single report may be of interest to many diverse audience groups, tailoring the reports to the individual interests of those different audience groups by putting a different cover sheet on and/or including a unique executive summary that highlights their interests or priorities might mean that the report gets read by different audiences without being rewritten fifteen different ways. In that case, the time taken to tailor the package would be time well spent. Some questions to help you decide whether a strategy or vehicle can be used with other audiences are provided in the following list.

Guiding Questions

- Will the headline or title appeal to or grab the attention of another audience group?
- Can we easily tailor the headline and first paragraph to better address another audience group?
- If there's "something for everyone," is it laid out in such a way that members of different audience groups can easily find what they're looking for?
- Do several audience groups read the same publication, listen to the same radio program, watch the same television program?

- Is this an event that would appeal to different audience groups? If yes, can we ensure that they are exposed to the messages most appropriate to their concerns?

STRATEGIES TO MATCH THE OBJECTIVE

Each communications objective is likely to require the implementation of several strategies before it is achieved. Ideally, strategies will build on each other, with the cumulative effect being the achievement of your objective. The following examples provide different strategies for three different communications objectives. (Obviously, there are dozens of strategies that could be considered for each of these objectives. The ones listed below are meant for discussion purposes only.) *Focal points* are strategies that some readers may be less familiar with or that suggest a new way of thinking about the strategies. They are meant to provide you with a quick overview. (If you are interested in learning more about a specific focal point, see the index for resource information.) Each example is followed by a brief discussion of the rationale used to analyze the appropriateness of these strategies using the seven criteria outlined previously.

CASE STUDY: FUTURE GENERATIONS

An important objective of the organization Future Generations is to inform 80 percent of all parents in School Districts 17, 19, 20, and 25 (the West Valley Region) about the effects of alcohol on adolescent development by the end of the school year. This first step is seen as a way to build awareness of the issue among a specific group of parents, laying the foundation for a more proactive commitment to alcohol abuse prevention efforts on a personal as well as a community level. Five possible strategies:

1. Conduct a series of evening forums with parent activists who can share their experiences as well as with experts to provide research findings and factual information; videotape the forums for playback on cable access television. On request, mail videotapes for home viewing (see *Focal Point: Cable Access*).

2. Send monthly mailings that will grab the attention of parents, highlighting the effects of alcohol on teens and a "talk to your kids"

guidesheet on the monthly topic (see *Focal Point: Print's Attention-Getters*).

3. Set up information tables at local grocery stores and/or neighborhood "strip malls"; recruit students to hand out leaflets and bumper stickers.

4. Have several students perform skits that present the issue dramatically at Fall-Winter PTA meetings.

5. Conduct training sessions about adolescents and alcohol abuse for junior high school teachers so that they can talk about the subject with parents during parent-teacher conferences (see *Focal Point: The Seminar/Workshop/Training Program*).

By considering how effective each strategy will be with this specific audience group, Future Generations staff will be able to evaluate and prioritize these strategies (see Exhibit 4-3).

Audience Responsiveness.   The majority of parents in the West Valley Region don't work in the evening, so they could be available to attend evening forums, parent/teacher conferences, and PTA meetings. During evening hours, parents are home with their families; therefore evening unconsciously becomes synonymous with "family time" and/or "family concerns."

With the level of cable households in the West Valley Region at 70 percent and VCR ownership matching the national average of 89 percent, those parents not able to attend the evening forums will have an opportunity to pick up the information through one of these two media. The viewing of the information will also take place in the home, again reinforcing the idea that these are "family concerns" that are being presented during "family time."

Monthly information packets via first-class mail are guaranteed to reach the parents in the home and can be read at each person's convenience. Along the same lines, leafleting at grocery stores and strip malls will again reach parents in an environment where they are likely to be engaged in personal and/or family concerns—for example, buying food for the family, picking up dry cleaning, toiletries, birthday cards, and so on. The interaction between adults and student activists will help ensure that the flyer gets at least a cursory glance. The problem, of course, with both of these strategies is: How likely is it that the material will be read? If possible, a feedback mechanism might be designed to help assess whether the information has been reviewed. A follow-up phone call or classroom assignment that requires the child to engage the parent in a discussion about one or several of the points made in the print materials might be needed for these strategies to be effective.

Exhibit 4-3 Analysis of Communications Strategy: Future Generations

Rating scale	1	2	3	4	5
Responsive to audience	**Highly responsive** Mail	Forums PTA meetings Parent/teacher		Leafleting	**Unresponsive**
Appropriate to relationship	**Very appropriate** Forums	PTA meetings Parent/teacher Mail	Leafleting		**Inappropriate**
Strategy affects perception	**Emotional** Parent/teacher	PTA meetings	Mail Forums	Leafleting	**Rational**
Strategy affects message	**Most control over message** Mail	Forums	Leafleting	PTA meetings Parent/teacher	**Least control**
Strategy affects message	**Most control over interpretation** Forums	PTA meetings	Parent/teacher Leafleting		**Least control** Mail
Effort to implement	**Least** Parent/teacher	PTA meetings	Mail	Leafleting	**Most** Forum
Cost to implement	Least expensive PTA meetings	Parent/teacher	Leafleting	Mail	Most expensive Forums
Impact on others	**Impact on others** Forum	Leafleting	PTA		**No impact** Parent/teacher Mail

	Responsiveness	Relationship	Perception (rational = 5)	Message control	Interpretation control	Effort to implement	Cost	Impact on others	Totals
Monthly mailings	1	2	3	1	5	3	4	5	26
Evening forums	2	1	3	2	1	5	5	1	22
Parent/teacher meetings	2	2	1	4	3	1	2	5	20
Leafleting	4	3	4	3	3	4	3	2	26
PTA meetings	2	2	2	4	2	2	1	3	18

What the score means

Monthly mailings   Scored low on interpretation control, cost, and impact on others

Evening forums   A lot of effort and cost involved; does that outweigh all the other positive factors?

Parent/teacher meetings   Low on message control and impact on others; cost-effective strategy

Leafleting   Not an exceptionally effective strategy—while no one area stands out as pro or con, it has the lowest score of all five strategies

PTA meetings   "Biggest bang for the buck"

Given the above, rank the strategies from most important to least important.

PTA meetings

Parent/teacher meetings

Evening forums

Monthly mailings

Leafleting

The Organization's Relationship to the Audience.   Future Generations is a twenty-five-year-old organization that has worked in the region to create healthy and safe communities, especially through its work with adolescents and teens. Approximately 50 percent of all parents in the West Valley Region have made a donation to the group over the past three years and approximately 25 percent have participated in the organization's programs either as teenagers or as adults. So, while Future Generations is not a "household word," it is generally well respected in the community as a credible and effective organization. Based on the organization's positive and proactive connection to the community, the evening forums, the monthly mailings, and the leaflets are more likely to be seen as valid, informed, and important—something to pay attention to.

The other two strategies—parent/teacher conferences and PTA meetings—rely more on the relationship of parents to the individual schools their children attend as well as on the relationship between Future Generations, the school districts, and individual schools, which has grown closer over the years. Attendance at fall-winter PTA meetings averages 25 to 50 percent in the different districts while, on average, approximately 70 percent of all students have at least one parent attend parent/teacher conferences during the fall semester. Thus, these strategies are appropriate given the relationship between the schools, parents, and Future Generations.

Strategy Influences Perceptions.   Because the evening forums as well as PTA meetings provide a chance for parents to socialize with each other and share mutual concerns, the audience is more likely to be relaxed and, thus, receptive to the message. In addition, the interactive nature of these strategies—as well as the intimacy of the parent-teacher conference—will help the audience better absorb the information because audience members will have the opportunity to talk about the information in the context of their own experience and ask questions to clarify their concerns and their thinking. In both of these strategies, the message is likelier to be perceived more rationally than emotionally.

Being approached by students in a shopping center or grocery store is also likely to not only catch the attention of a parent but also suggest some urgency. The fact, however, that the audience's attention is focused on "other business" may quickly neutralize that perception. A dramatic portrayal by students of an issue that concerns them and their future success is also likely to move parents on an emotional level, making them more emotionally receptive to the message even as it is discussed afterward.

And, while a first-class mailing may convey a certain urgency and importance, it is also likely to be read and perceived more rationally than emotionally. Another perception problem that may be encountered with this strategy is that, because of the heavy volume of mail most households receive, another piece, even if sent first class, may be more easily dismissed than a face-to-face encounter of any kind. The writing and design of the print pieces are likely to influence the perception of the message very much more so in the mailed piece than in the leaflet, because the mailed piece doesn't have the benefit of a personal delivery scheme.

The Strategy Affects the Message. In all of these strategies, Future Generations has control of the message with the target audience to one degree or another. In the monthly mailings as well as in the leaflets, it has total control over what is said and how it is expressed. It is more difficult, however, to control the message as it gets interpreted and delivered by the student volunteers. While the organization can train the volunteers on what the issues are and on what they should say when approaching people, it can't guarantee that every student volunteer will follow that formula.

Along similar lines, Future Generations staff can brief the teachers and bring them up to speed on the issues, but there can be no guarantee as to which issues or concerns the parents will raise in private conversations, to which the teachers will have to respond.

In the same way, the strategy can influence the dramatization by the students but, in order for it to be authentic and "ring true," the presentation must be the students' interpretation of the message. The organization can, on the other hand, guide the discussion afterward to some degree and, again, choose an appropriate staff person to answer questions that might arise during the discussion time as a way of clarifying and controlling the message. The forum, another public meeting that consists of a program followed by discussion, gives the organization slightly more control over the message because the organization can choose experts who will reinforce the message the organization wishes to send. (If the press is targeted to cover the forum, however, the organization will have less control over how the message is interpreted by and presented in the press.)

Effort to Implement. Each strategy varies in the amount of staff time needed to make it happen. The evening forum, along with taping the session and distributing it through the mail and on cable access, plus preparing materials to give to participants to take home afterward, is the most staff-intensive strategy of the five suggested here. The parent/teacher meetings would take the least amount of effort, since the organization would only have to brief the teachers once, which it could do through available print and video materials.

If necessary, this could be followed by an audioconference so that the organization's staff could answer more specific questions the teachers might have.

The student skits at PTA meetings would take fewer organizational resources than the leafleting project, since a single staff person could be available on an as-needed basis to work on preparing the skits. Coordinating and educating a cadre of students to do the outreach; preparing the leaflets, bumper stickers, table signs, and so forth; and getting permission to distribute leaflets at various commercial sites would take a good deal more time and attention. At the midpoint would be the monthly mailing, which would have to be written, produced, collated, and mailed every month.

Budget Issues.   In addition to staff time, financial concern often is the deciding factor for many nonprofits engaged in planning strategies that will effectively create social change. The least expensive strategies would be the PTA meeting and the parent/teacher conferences, since these would require a minimum of print handouts to use as take-home materials. Expenses for the leafleting strategy would be just above the other two, the main cost being the production of the leaflets, bumper stickers, and table signs. The monthly mailings would be the next most costly. One first-class monthly mailing, sending a self-mailer piece to 7500 homes, would cost approximately $3000–$4500. Three such mailings would cost $9,000–$13,500. On the high end would be the evening forums—hall rentals, speakers' travel, promotional expenses, videotape production expenses, handouts, and so on. A series of four forums could easily cost $30,000–$50,000.

Potential Impact on Other Audience Groups.   The likelihood of a mailing reaching individuals beyond those in the household itself would not be expected, nor would it be counted on. Thus, this strategy is unlikely to have an impact on other audience groups. (This is not to say that the same materials or selected pieces from these mailings couldn't be used to brief reporters, local policy makers, educators, or others.) Similarly, the parent/teacher meetings are private, confidential conversations between two or three people. This strategy is also unlikely to have an impact on individuals beyond the people involved in the conversation. Adequately preparing teachers to handle the matter during parent/teacher meetings, however, will build awareness of the issue among teachers, principals, guidance counselors, and others who work within the school system while helping them work through the issues involved, perhaps turning them into advocates among parents and students with whom they work.

In addition to the students who become involved in the PTA skits or the leafleting effort, the other three strategies—the PTA meetings, the leafleting, and the evening forums—could have an impact on other, less directly involved audiences. Reporters might be interested in covering one or all of these events, local policy makers might be interested in attending the evening forums or reading the highlights of what experts said, and small business owners might become more aware of the issue due to the leafleting that is happening right outside their doors.

Focal Point: Cable Access

In some communities, cable access—also known as public access—television plays an important role in the local communications environment. There are as many reasons for this as there are differences in the communities that have this service, but the most frequently cited are:

- It gives ordinary citizens and organizations that would otherwise not have access to the mass media a chance to be heard. Public access gives the organization complete control of the content—there are very few content restrictions for cable access.

- Production and distribution costs are usually free or fairly affordable because community access facilities are usually funded through a fee the cable company pays the city or town for access to public rights-of-way. This makes it possible for individuals and organizations to produce programming at a cost they can afford.

- Targeted populations can be reached on a regular basis, especially if there is enough publicity telling audiences that the program exists and has a permanent time slot that viewers can regularly tune in to.

- Many public access centers provide an opportunity for staff and volunteers to learn how to produce video programming, a skill that can be used both for programs on the cable access channel and for video messages that the organization may want to distribute to key constituencies. (An organization can also hire an independent producer to create the program and still get free airtime for showing the videotape.)

- Programs can be repeated, which increases the likelihood of having more people from your target audience group actually see the programs. Word of mouth within distinct populations is often the best promotion for a cable access program!

Who watches cable access? It depends on the community as well as individual programs and the effort put into promoting those programs to the target audience. Because cable access gives an organization the chance to deliver a powerful visual message to a target population—with the chances that the program will go much beyond that population virtually nil—programs can employ messages and images that resonate most strongly with those target populations, regardless of the fact that other populations might not relate to the message at all. For example, a program aimed at Hispanics with diabetes or gay men with HIV could provide very frank information, case histories, health tips, and the like, which would be of little interest to people outside the target population. Yet, through television, an organization might be able to deliver its message in a forceful way by selecting powerful images, moving personal stories, and answers to questions viewers might have about their own situations—not something that occurs regularly on broadcast television or even on radio! The key to this strategy is not only to produce the program but to get the word out to the target audience that the program can be seen at a certain time on a certain channel. If your organization decides to produce a regular series—whether weekly or monthly—it can better cultivate a following within the target population and generate word-of-mouth recommendations from viewers to others in the population.

In addition to serving the organization's constituents and the community at large, cable access can also result in a higher profile for the organization's services and (if it is an advocacy organization) for its position on issues of importance to the community. If the organization is linked closely to the program content, viewers will come to know the organization and begin seeing it as a resource and a vital feature of the community.

Focal Point: Print's Attention-Getters

Seven elements are used to grab the attention of the individual to whom a print piece is targeted. By recognizing the effect of each element on an individual—both consciously and unconsciously—your organization can better use and combine these for the greatest impact.

1. *Photos.* A picture is worth a thousand words. A photo is purely visual and, more often than not, it grabs an individual's attention before anything else on a print piece, even the headlines. We can easily get a sense of what is happening, what the story or message is about, simply by looking at a photo. A photo is "real" in a way that a drawing or painting is not.

2. *Photo captions and pull quotes.* Captions with pictures are read 70 percent more frequently than all other copy. Pull quotes—highlighted ideas without pictures—often are used to reinforce key points or ideas, giving someone skimming through a piece a sort of "executive summary." Frequently, one or two catchy pull quotes may be the deciding factor for someone who is unsure whether he or she should take the time to read something in its entirety.

> Captions with pictures are read 70 percent more frequently than all other copy.

3. *Headlines/Titles.* Boldness and brevity capture a reader's attention in a few seconds while conveying the essence of the story in a nutshell. *The Body as Battlefield* or *Let's Make a Doctor or Let's Make a Deal* are two headlines that do this extremely well. If the headline doesn't "sing" to the reader, he or she won't look at the rest of the piece.

4. *Design.* If a piece looks interesting, it is likely to pique someone's curiosity. If a piece is designed so that it is easy to read, it is more likely to be read. If a piece is unusual in its size, shape, or weight, it is more likely to be noticed when it is picked up, even if it is one of many print pieces vying for the individual's attention.

5. *Sidebars/boxes.* Separating key points in a document and setting them off from the main text guides a reader's eye to that segment of text because readers know it encapsulates the important elements of the longer piece. These blocked pieces of text are also used to attach related material as well as to make a long piece appear shorter.

6. *Graphs and charts.* Often this type of visual representation is used to emphasize and simplify a key message or point that is based on statistics by compressing numerical data into an efficient visual form. Graphs and charts help readers more readily understand what the numbers mean (see Exhibit 4-4).

7. *Color.* Market research as well as psychological study has been done about the impact of color on the human nervous system. People unconsciously respond to color, and the meanings given to certain colors are constantly reinforced by our culture—for example, red is associated with anger, heat, energy; blue is interpreted as cool, calm, stable; green represents envy as well as environmental concerns. In a world defined by words—where black and white is the standard because it is easy for the eyes to focus on over a long period of time—color can be used to call attention to a message or reinforce a theme.

Exhibit 4-4 Communications Allocations

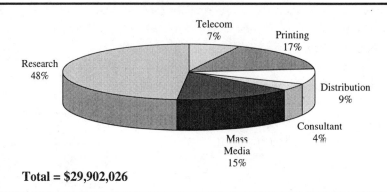

Total = $29,902,026

Focal Point: The Seminar/Workshop/Training Program

Rarely understood as a communications strategy, this type of program can bring participants through all four communications objective quadrants in a single session. It has a unique structure—like a conference, it has a set agenda and a moderator, and information is presented, although usually not in such a static way as it is at a conference. However, the seminar also shares qualities with a briefing in that it is more free-flowing, and people become engaged in a conversation or discussion much more easily than at a conference; there is more of an idea exchange. For example, a communications workshop with a daylong agenda might have a few interactive presentations on some of the relevant topics during which the large group not only gets new information but solves problems as a group. This might be interspersed with small break-out group exercises during which individuals work on plans for their own organization, followed by a chance for participants to share information and get feedback on their work. The goal of this type of educational program is to give the participants something to walk away with—usually something that is practical and useful to them in their day-to-day lives. This is usually not true in a conference or after a briefing.

Because this type of educational program usually begins with the provision of new information in a way that will grab the participants' attention, the session immediately sets out to build awareness among the audience about the subject or issue on which the session is focused.

Once that is set in motion, participants are quickly moved forward and begin working through their thoughts and opinions about the matter as way to encourage them to act on the information as it is presented within the learning environment. Because the educational experience involves not only interaction between the trainer and the participants but also among the participants, relationships are likely to begin to take shape by the end of the program.

This type of educational program excels in accomplishing these four objectives when it provides an opportunity for participants to engage in open discussion, experiential learning, and unstructured time to network and share information with each other.

By the end of the session, common ground has been established between the workshop leader, the host organization, and the participants which frequently results in a further relationship because it is perceived as being mutually beneficial to all involved. However, it is usually the leader or the host organization that must nurture such relationships if they are to truly evolve over time.

CASE STUDY: SHELTER FROM THE STORM

Shelter from the Storm, a national nonprofit organization that acts as the advocacy voice for 100 local agencies around the country that provide services to victims of domestic violence, wants to secure commitments from ten senior legislators to not only sponsor but also champion a proactive public policy initiative that will provide new resources to address the problem of domestic violence. The target audience will be senior legislators—possibly a few dozen individuals from among whom staff will select the final ten and move them toward a deeper commitment to the cause. This will require engaging these audience members in a dialogue or deliberation process that will convince them of the problem and the public policy solution being proposed. Possible strategies might include:

1. Conduct three breakfast briefings—one in New York for magazine editors, the second in Washington, DC for a select group of reporters who cover Capitol Hill, and the third for interested legislative staff. Feature two experts who will discuss new research findings due out next month. Invite two activists who have suffered from domestic violence in the past to talk about the human side of the story. Conduct one-on-one follow-up (phone and visits) to assess commitment to engaging readers/legislators further (see *Focal Point: The Briefing*).

2. Match key business leaders who support the cause with legislators using the representative's fund-raising records, family acquaintances, business interests, or mutual acquaintances. Provide supporters with talking points and schedule a series of legislative visits so that they

can engage the legislators in a serious discussion about the issue and the reasons for the proposed policy. Debrief afterward with staff. Set up one-on-one interviews between business supporters and DC press and/or business press.

3. Conduct a national audioconference to inform local supporters about the issue and legislative effort so that they can attend community meetings when the policy maker is in his or her home district to pose the question of sponsorship; provide press with background information after the meeting (see *Focal Point: The Audio conference*).

4. Place an op-ed piece in local newspapers that covers the policy makers' districts; forward reprints to legislators and senior staff (see *Focal Point: Print Vehicles Controlled by the Mass Media Establishment*).

5. For the month prior to legislative recess, place thirty-second radio spots featuring an 800 number that gets routed to representatives' office in Washington, DC (see *Focal Point: Radio Environment; Focal Point: Smart Routing*).

6. Post comments to appropriate usenets and listservs to encourage readers to send e-mail to the targeted policy makers (see *Focal Point: Online Discussion Groups*).

Expected Audience Responsiveness to Strategy. Two strategies will directly engage the legislators—the meetings with business leaders and discussions they will have with their staff after the legislative briefing. Both strategies rely on the fact that the key audience—legislators—will be open to engaging in this type of discussion with these two "outreach partners." In selecting business leaders as the organization's emissaries, the staff hopes to ensure that the issue is seen as critical and serious—and not simply as an "emotional" issue. Obviously, legislative staff will also have the ability to engage their legislator in thinking through the proposed policy and have a strong influence on the end result.

Shelter from the Storm staff members also recognize the influence that the press has on individual legislators and legislation as well as on setting the policy agenda—another strategy to which the target audience will naturally respond. Because of this, the press briefings are meant to inform a select group of reporters in such a way that they will pursue the issue not just as a single news story but, hopefully, as a series of articles where the issue unfolds slowly and over time.

The staff also knows that legislators are responsive to issues when voters express concern about those issues—either at meetings "back home" or via phone calls to congressional offices. For this reason, having the message repeated in the legislators' home districts via radio spots, speakers at community meetings where press coverage is likely, and op-eds in the local paper also will help open the door to greater consideration of the matter by the legislators.

Finally, while the staff doesn't expect the legislators themselves to read their e-mail, the legislative staff members continuously count the number of people who speak out for or against an issue, whether they do so via mail, phone, fax, or e-mail. The organization hopes to generate a large volume of e-mail messages as a way to demonstrate widespread support for the proposed policy.

The Organization's Relationship to the Audience. While Shelter from the Storm has a staff person assigned to Capitol Hill and another who concentrates on grassroots organizing, the organization has no more than average name recognition and clout as it works to distinguish itself from among hundreds of advocacy groups based in Washington, DC. The suggested strategies reflect that fact and rely on the organization's relationship with others who will have a more direct influence on the legislators.

Shelter from the Storm does have good working relationships with many reporters in both Washington and New York, and it is recognized as a reliable source for factual information as well as for its ability to find credible individuals who help "humanize" stories.

In addition, a key board member is the chairman of a Fortune 500 company and has used his contacts to introduce the organization to dozens of his colleagues, many of whom have expressed a willingness to help out when the right time arose. Most of these individuals have personal and/or professional relationships with members in the target audience.

Finally, Shelter from the Storm can tap its local service network to sponsor the radio spots in the local market yet produce a single spot with a single 800 number for follow-up. These local groups will also be able to recommend local supporters who could attend community meetings and ask the hard questions. And Shelter from the Storm has a dozen volunteers who monitor usenets, subscribe to relevant listservs, and post to various Web sites in order to build "relationships" with others who subscribe to and participate in these electronic forums.

Strategy Influences Perceptions. Because the organization is trying to elicit the proactive support of senior legislators for the proposed public policy, it is important that the matter be presented in a rational, objective, and businesslike manner. By taking this approach, the legislators who do become allies will have facts and research analysis on which to "hang their hat," not simply feelings, which can easily be challenged or changed. When it is time to move the legislation forward—once it is scheduled for committee hearings, for example—the organization will begin to mobilize key constituent groups, creating an emotional groundswell for the issue.

The first three strategies rely on human interaction—face-to-face meetings of one sort or another. Briefings, by their very nature, are more informal, a presentation of background information and analysis, a place where ideas are exchanged and attitudes are often easy to read. Briefings do not suggest the urgency of a press release or a press event, for example, and because of this, participants can take the time needed to assimilate the information more rationally than emotionally.

The same would be true at a meeting between constituent and legislator on Capitol Hill, which is at once formal yet intimate. In a conversation, the individual's body language can be read and eye contact can be made to reinforce the sincerity and/or the attitude of the individuals at the meeting. These meetings are likely to explore the issue from a more rational perspective than, for example, meetings between policy makers and women who had lived through domestic violence, which would have the potential of exploring the issue in a more emotional way and possibly generating a more emotional or visceral response.

Community meetings generate a different atmosphere than the other two types of face-to-face strategies in that people from the community—neighbors, friends, people whose children go to the same schools, and so forth—come together to discuss issues that they see as important. Often these meetings have an emotional edge, because the issues "hit home" with the people in the audience while the legislator knows that his or her job is directly influenced by the attitudes and opinions of these voters—the people who take the time to participate in community meetings and become involved in their communities.

Op-eds, a print strategy, can combine the emotional side of an issue with a more rational approach; however, due to the brevity of most op-eds, this is not an easy task. Most op-eds take an either/or approach—either they confront an issue objectively, using research or historical facts, polling data, social indicators, and the like to make their case, or the issue is discussed from a more human, emotional point of view. Radio spots can also create an emotional context for the facts because not only does the voice color the issue but what is said is limited to 30 seconds and thus must be more forceful, persuasive, and to-the-point than a print piece.

Electronic mail messages are more "disembodied" and the organization's staff doesn't expect an emotional response to the messages that will be generated. Again, the "counting" to be done by the legislator and his or her staff means that this strategy is most likely to have a more rational reception by the target audience.

The Strategy Affects the Message.   The organization has direct control over how the message is discussed in the op-ed piece and delivered in the radio spots but, because human interaction is an essential part of the other strategies, the organization's control over the message varies considerably.

By reinforcing a specific framing of the issue and sticking to key talking points, the staff can hope to control how the message initially is put before the key audience and the groups it has decided to work with as "outreach partners." But, in any briefing, participants expect to have their questions answered, and those questions may steer the discussion away from the message points the organization wants to have stressed when the outreach partners leave the briefing.

Because of the nature of the briefing strategy, the end result—whether news or feature articles or a report back to the legislator by his or her staff member—is beyond the organization's control (although it can respond to representations made in the press through letters to the editor, it is unlikely that the organization will ever know what information was transmitted between the staff member and the legislator).

While the organization can brief the business leaders about key issues, facts, and personal stories as well as provide them with talking points, once the business leader is in the meeting it will be impossible to ensure that the message stays intact. But having a discussion with a peer (in terms of power within each of their respective worlds) will better help ensure that the legislator becomes truly engaged in thinking through the issue.

In a similar way, a local supporter who brings up the issue at the community meeting may state the message exactly as the organization might wish, but follow-up questions and discussions that involve other members of the community will be beyond the control of the local supporter and the organization. Indeed, opposing points of view are just as likely as not to arise from the introduction of the issue in this type of forum.

Finally, the e-mail strategy is a blend of message control. While the volunteers obviously control the message that they send out, keeping it true to the organization's framing, how that message gets interpreted and "spun" by others who will (hopefully) send messages to policy makers is beyond the organization's control; it is not likely the organization will ever know what was said by whom.

Effort to Implement.   The necessary expertise can be found among staff and volunteers, but the most time-consuming strategy to implement will be the briefings—contacting the invitees, preparing the researchers and the spokes-women, creating the materials to hand out to the press, doing the follow-up phone calls. The least time-consuming for the organization will be generating the e-mail messages, especially since this will be handled almost entirely by volunteers. Writing and placing the op-ed piece and generating the e-mail messages will probably take a similar amount of time for development and distribution. Recruiting and briefing the business leaders and local support-ers will take a good deal of staff time, but the end result is anticipated to be a major factor in helping the organization achieve its objective.

Budget Issues.   All of these strategies are fairly inexpensive when staff time is not factored into the equation (see the preceding paragraph). While audio pro-duction is affordable, placement of the radio spots in the local markets so as to saturate the ten target markets for a two- to three-week period of time during the morning and afternoon hours—the time when female supporters are most likely to listen and call—will be expensive. The briefings will be at the high end—with out-of-pocket costs for breakfasts and a private room as well as travel for the two researchers and the two women who will represent the expe-rience of domestic violence. The business leaders have agreed to cover their own travel expenses, and the e-mail strategy costs virtually nothing since the volunteers pay their own Internet access charges. The only other item that will cost money will be the print materials for the press and legislative staff, the "leave behinds" for the legislators, and the cost of reprints and postage to dis-tribute the op-eds.

Potential Impact on Other Audience Groups.   All of these strategies will have an impact on other audiences—most notably, those audience groups who will act as "outreach partners"—the press, legislative staff, business leaders, local community supporters, and online supporters—because they will be actively engaged in discussing the issue.

In addition, the press briefings will (hopefully) have a ripple effect with readers/viewers of the news media over time. Although it is unlikely that it will be enough exposure—or the depth of coverage that is needed—to result in actually engaging the public in deliberating on the issue in all of its complexity, individuals who get their news from those media that do sto-ries as a result of the briefing will at the least become aware of the issue. This will be reinforced by the op-ed, follow-up letters to the editor gener-ated by the op-ed, and the radio spots.

Focal Point: The Briefing

A briefing is a more informal face-to-face gathering, but it is also carefully orchestrated by the host organization. A briefing is held less to talk to attendees than to engage them in a conversation about a specific topic. While the host organization supplies the experts who lead off the discussion, present the issue, and provide the facts, the primary objective is to elicit from the participants their concerns or questions about an issue, which are then addressed and clarified so that a dialogue among the participants and the host ensues. In this way, a more personal connection is likely to be made between the issue and the participants.

Because of their informality, briefings are excellent in helping participants work through an issue and have been used successfully in grabbing the attention of participants about an issue of which they were previously unaware. At the same time, briefings can be used to initiate relationships or to strengthen existing relationships.

Focal Point: The Audioconference

Conference calling is a cost-effective way to conduct small to medium-size meetings—that is, less than twelve people. The more people on the call, the greater the need for a structured agenda and guidelines for participants—for example, requiring participants to identify themselves before speaking, using a moderator to manage participants who want to speak at the same time, and so on. This type of conference call has been used to help an audience work through issues (although not as effectively as face-to-face strategies) and, like all phone applications, it can be a powerful tool for building and strengthening relationships.

Given the increased mobility of our population, a new way to manage a conference call is now available. Instead of an operator calling everyone at previously agreed-upon phone numbers, participants are given a phone number beforehand to call into the conference. In this way, everyone can participate from wherever he or she happens to be—an airport, someone else's office, or a hotel room.

This call-in technology has made it possible to use a conference call as a way to narrowcast programs—think closed-circuit radio. Some callers—the speakers—have the capacity to speak and listen to anyone else on the call, while others, who are given a different number to call, have listen-only capacity. It is possible, however, for the listeners to interact with the speakers by using the touch-tone pad to signal the operator that they would like to speak.

The telephone company operator (often called the conference coordinator) acknowledges that person and "turns on" his or her phone line so that he or she can engage in a conversation, for a limited time, with the speakers.

This application has been used successfully by nonprofits in the following circumstances:

- For informational programs aimed at targeted audiences like high-dollar donors or activists
  - Thirty of the organization's high-dollar donors listen to a briefing originating from Geneva, where program staff members are participating in an international summit on human rights.
- For press conferences
  - An organization invites experts from Milwaukee, Seattle, Detroit, and Boston to talk to national reporters (primarily in New York and Washington) about the impact that welfare reform is having on their communities.
- For training staff, volunteers, or members
  - The first Monday of every month, a program is offered during lunchtime to clarify a new environmental policy to local activists who will be monitoring enforcement in their communities.
- For briefing coalition members across the country on strategic plans
  - A month before a national poll is released on the public's attitudes toward children, a program is held so the pollster can explain the results. This is followed by presentations by four members on their plans for the upcoming mobilization. Local groups are gathered together to listen to the program on speakerphones. Afterward, local activists remain together at the local sites to discuss their strategies.

While this application has proven to be a cost-effective way of building awareness of an issue among targeted audiences as well as strengthening relationships, it is not particularly useful if the purpose is to help people work through difficult issues, because it doesn't allow free-flowing conversation among participants as a traditional conference call or face-to-face meeting would.

Focal Point: Print Vehicles Controlled by the Mass Media Establishment

Anytime you entrust your message to someone outside the organization, you must carefully consider beforehand how that messenger will deliver the message and the nature of the relationship of the messenger to its audience, because that relationship will affect how the audience interprets the message. A news story in *The Washington Post* will be perceived—and received—differently than a story on the same subject in *The Village Voice* or *The Catholic Herald*. Similarly, *Time* or *Newsweek* will report a story on AIDS through a different lens than *The Atlantic Monthly*, *Woman's Health*, or *The Advocate*. Knowing the messenger's audience as well as the messenger's own editorial perspective on your issues can enable your organization to succeed not only in "placing the story," but, more importantly, in having the story told in a way that reflects your organization's core message to that targeted audience.

The best way to figure out why any print publication—whether daily or weekly newspapers, magazines, or journals—would be interested in your organization and/or its issues is to read several editions, noting not just which reporters are covering what stories, but also how the stories are reported. This will tell you not only about the editorial perspective of the newspaper or magazine and its reporters—whether staff or freelance—but, more importantly, how the readers' opinions, attitudes, and beliefs are being influenced (positively or negatively) by the way the issues are presented—what is being covered, what facts are included, which are left out, and so on.

Most morning daily newspapers play an agenda-setting role for the rest of the media in that media market—that is, the afternoon and early evening broadcast news often takes its story lineup from that morning's daily newspaper. This gives that particular print vehicle even more clout than its mere readership would suggest—in 1997, 50 percent of all American adults indicated that they had read a newspaper in a given week. This can be a critical reason for pursuing a print reporter or editor of your daily newspaper—even to the point of offering that person an exclusive to your news story. At the same time, however, an organization must be ready to follow up on any coverage in the daily newspaper in a variety of ways—whether through additional (and ongoing) press outreach or with organizationally produced media targeted to specific constituencies. A single mention of your issue or organization in the daily newspaper may set the wheels in motion, but your organization must have a plan and be prepared to keep pedaling if it wishes to keep awareness of the issue alive and build momentum, which will hopefully result in resolution of the issue or problem over time.

Weekly or alternative newspapers are rapidly increasing their readership and tend to have more feature stories but less time-sensitive news. Aimed at very targeted communities—whether defined geographically, by shared interests, or by a common culture—this medium can help an organization get attention for an issue or event that directly concerns the community served by the weekly. Furthermore, it is usually easier to get the attention of reporters, freelance writers, and editors at a weekly or alternative paper because of such papers' targeted coverage and limited ability to go out into the community to "find" news. Some organizations also have arrangements with weeklies to write a regular feature, which in turn has helped those organizations build and maintain their relationships with the communities served by the weeklies.

Once an issue has been covered in a weekly or an alternative press, you may be able to create interest among other media outlets that serve other communities or that have a broader service area, such as the daily newspaper, radio, television, or cable television news outlets. But be prepared to answer the following: "Why should I report this? It's already been done."

Finally, magazines are an excellent way to build awareness of an organization and its issues among targeted audiences, and in some cases can move those audiences to act. Most magazines attract narrowly defined audiences made up mostly of regular subscribers. Once an organization has identified the audience(s) that is critical to its efforts, it can easily pick and choose the magazines members of such groups read. Once the target list of magazines is compiled, the organization must go about cultivating a relationship with the editorial staff and regular writers—many of whom may be freelance and might help you pitch your story to the magazine. This makes it easier for an organization to target those audiences that are critical to its efforts.

Focal Point: The Radio Environment

While each radio station has its own personality and mix of programs that distinguish it within its community of service—all news, easy listening, country and western, talk radio, news and commentary shows, special interest programs—another factor to consider is the type of radio environment your audience experiences. Each has advantages and disadvantages.

Urban markets.   There are dozens of radio stations and programming options available in most urban markets. If all the stations were taken into consideration, it is likely that they would, as a whole, represent the diverse populations within the urban community of service. However, when looked at individually, radio in an urban market is very fragmented, which makes it more akin to narrowcasting—reaching smaller, well defined audiences—than to broadcasting—a mass medium with a wider reach that uses a "lower common denominator" in programming the station so as to be popular with more people of diverse interests and experiences (rather than fewer people with common interests.)

Smaller Markets and Rural Areas.   There are many fewer radio stations on the air in these markets, which means that each will have a greater share of the entire market although the actual number of listeners may be substantially less than for any station in an urban market. For organizations working in rural communities, a radio station is synonymous with "mass media"—true broadcasting capability. To reach a specific audience—teens, parents, farmers, retirees, and so on—an organization would be better off studying the audience profile for specific programs to choose those that have a following among those listeners.

Syndicated Networks.   There are dozens of syndicated radio networks and syndicated radio shows. These syndicated programs have had a large impact on the nature of local radio service because when a station broadcasts a syndicated program, it is broadcasting something that did not originate within the community and thus does not reflect the local nature of the community the station serves. The more syndicated shows, the less responsiveness to the unique concerns and culture of the community. Yet, a program heard in thirty, forty, or fifty cities across the country can have a tremendous influence on the national agenda. This has become especially true with nationally syndicated talk radio shows, where the opinions of a few are heard by millions of listeners throughout the country. Public interest groups from the right, left, and center have used talk radio with mixed success. This is because the audience—especially the callers, who can be quite blunt when expressing their opinions, which are often one-sided or controversial (that's why they get on the air)—determines the direction of the program and, unless you've "seeded" the field with your own advocates who can ask the questions you want to answer, this is a factor very much under the control of the program's producer or host. Finding the answer as to "what's in it for them"—higher ratings, controversy, public service—is key to preparing for your issue or a spokesperson from your organization to be featured on these programs.[1]

The audiences for these programs are meticulously delineated by the syndicate. Ask for the information by contacting the syndicate directly, or review trade publications such as *Broadcasting Yearbook*.

Focal Point: Smart Routing

The telephone company's computer switch reads every telephone call's incoming and outgoing phone number. This is how calls are routed from one

---

[1] For more detailed information, see Pat Auferheide and Jeff Chester, *Talk Radio*, the Center for Strategic Communications/the Benton Foundation, 1992.

place to another, making sure that the bill goes to the number from which the call originated. By programming the computer switch, a phone company can route the call to another number that has been designated by the recipient for one reason or another. Indeed, this is how the popular call forwarding service is managed. Smart routing takes this principle to the next level, giving organizations the opportunity to route calls placed to a single 800 number to different destinations depending on criteria such as:

- Area code or the first three digits of a phone number (to route to the location nearest the caller)
  - An agency promotes a single number, but callers are transferred to the clinic nearest them so they can make an appointment.
- Zip codes that the caller enters via the touch-tone pad
  - Individuals call a single number about pending legislation and, after a brief message, are transferred to their congressional representative.
- Hour of day the call is placed
  - A national organization with regional offices can answer calls from 7:30 A.M. to 10:30 P.M. eastern time, with the East Coast office taking the first five hours, the Midwest office answering for the next five hours, and the last five hours being covered by the West Coast office, whose staff leaves at 7:30 P.M. Pacific time.
- An individual's home or office number, which that person has entered via the touch-tone pad to signal the telephone company's computer switch that he or she is "on duty" and can accept forwarded calls
  - An organization can use more volunteers to handle calls to a hotline or a management advice line without having to pay for additional phones and office space because volunteers can work from their homes or offices.

The biggest advantage of this strategy is that it allows an organization to promote a single number while maximizing available human resources. Along the way, the phone number becomes synonymous with the organization, building awareness of the organization and its services. It can also be a powerful tool in getting people to act—making an appointment, talking to a legislative assistant, or finding shelter for the night—because only one call needs to be made.

Focal Point: Online Discussion Groups

There are several ways to set up and conduct online discussion groups. Each method has its own advantages and disadvantages. The three primary methods used are listservs, Internet relay chats, and usenets.

Listservs are facilitated through electronic mailing lists in which anyone with an Internet e-mail address can participate. This electronic mailing list is stored in a computer that automatically distributes any messages sent to it to everyone who is on the electronic mailing list. To join a listserv, a person sends an e-mail message to the listserv's e-mail address. In the body of the text, he or she types *subscribe [name of the listserv]*. The person then receives an automatic reply from the listserv computer, confirming that he or she has been registered for the listserv and explaining in more detail what the discussion is about and whether there are any rules for participants to follow in posting messages to the discussion. Anytime someone sends a message to the listserv, the listserv computer automatically forwards that message to everyone on the list, creating a community of interest among the participants.

Listservs exist for hundreds of purposes. People subscribe to listservs to discuss the latest trends or research with colleagues, to get information, and to engage in conversation on matters of mutual interest. Some listservs are moderated, while others are not. Because listservs use e-mail technology, the conversation doesn't happen in real time, which means subscribers can participate at their convenience. Plus, individuals who don't have Internet access but have e-mail addresses—which is a substantial number of people—have a chance to participate in the discussion as well.

A second method for conducting online discussion is through a program called Internet relay chat (IRC), better known as "chat." This allows participants to "talk" to each other in real time. Unlike listservs, users must be logged into a specific computer network to participate in a chat group. Participants in chat discussions create or go to a "chat room," which is like a closed channel where anything anyone types is seen by all others on that channel, allowing for a discussion among multiple participants. (There are also ways to be in the chat room and select messages to be seen only by one of the participants.)

There are thousands of chat groups on the Internet, covering a wide range of personal and professional interests. While the conversation happens in real time and can be more fluid, it does require Internet access and patience if participants are slow typists—which makes the conversation move more slowly.

The third way to set up an online discussion is through a usenet, a worldwide electronic bulletin board system on the Internet where visitors who are interested in a specific topic post messages to "discussions," which are also known as newsgroups. The posted information is available to anyone connected to the Internet who "stops by" to read what's there. Because of this, usenets have the potential to attract random users as well as regular visitors.

Unlike chat groups, usenet newsgroups do not require that participants come together at the same time, so participants can check in at their convenience, stay as long as they like, and read as much as they want. Because the discussion isn't moderated, individuals can post comments or questions of any length.

CASE STUDY: PLANET 3000

Planet 3000 is a nonprofit research and advocacy group. One of its communications objectives is to mobilize small business owners from seventy-five congressional districts (representatives considered "swing" votes) in the Northeast and Midwest to support a comprehensive transportation/clean air policy initiative. Some strategies the staff is considering include:

1. Conduct a poll to assess depth of support for this type of policy among the targeted audience group and how far members of the group are willing to support it. Release findings at a press conference held in conjunction with National Chambers of Commerce Annual Meeting (see *Focal Point: The Conference*).

2. Distribute radio actualities and VNRs highlighting the poll findings, the impact of traffic on air quality, the policy initiative, and the chambers' involvement. Provide a list of local campaign coordinators to media outlets as well (see *Focal Point: Radio Actualities; Focal Point: Video News Releases*).

3. Recruit a "celebrity" spokesperson to present at the National Chambers of Commerce Annual Meeting in Washington, DC. Do a satellite media tour to piggyback on the chambers' "lobby day" held in conjunction with the Annual Meeting. Have a booth in the exhibit area and sign up local chambers of commerce from these districts to become sponsors of the Planet 3000 "business for business" campaign where one small business owner enlists the support of another. Draft and design a commitment pledge and an engagement package that the chambers can use to launch the campaign with their members (see *Focal Point: Satellite Media Tours*).

4. Create a home page for the "business for business" campaign with links to local groups in the seventy-five targeted districts. Feature weekly updates using "real audio" messages from local activists and our celebrity spokesperson. Highlight specific businesses using Adobe Acrobat files so that local groups and businesses can download the files and place them in their local newsletters, flyers, posters, and so on (see *Focal Point: Why Use the World Wide Web*).

5. Fax broadcast a policy analysis to key business press contacts and hold an audio conference with key experts to answer specific questions. Offer local spokespersons to provide a local angle and/or "human interest" side of the story (see *Focal Point: Delivery and Distribution Messages*).

Expected Audience Responsiveness to the Strategy.   The first strategy will not only help staff assess the target audience's opinion more accurately but, when combined with the second strategy, can help generate attention for the issue with local reporters and media outlets in the targeted districts. The local press has a direct influence on small business owners as well as on congressional representatives from those districts because the daily newspapers and radio and television news broadcasts create the environment within which business owners do business.

Planet 3000 staff members expect the target audience to be more responsive to the message because it will have the imprimatur of the chambers of commerce that traditionally serve their interests. At the same time, the National Chambers of Commerce will welcome a celebrity spokesperson as a way to lend cachet to its annual meeting without any effort on its part.

Faxing out a policy analysis to the business press—a reputable source of information for small business owners—ensures that the target audience will be more readily persuaded by these messengers. Enlisting the support of these "outreach partners" means that members of the target audience will be reached through the vehicles with which they are already familiar during the time of day when their minds are on business concerns.

Finally, by linking a Web site strategy to the effort, the staff hopes to create a national movement that connects all the local efforts and supporters visually as well as through shared information and through national recognition of efforts at the local level. Plus, this creation of an online resource that can easily be downloaded by local organizations who can then "drop" graphically designed files into newsletters and leaflets, creating new information on a regular basis at no cost to develop, will help ensure that updates are sent regularly to local supporters even if they do not have access to the Internet.

The Organization's Relationship to the Audience.   Planet 3000 does not have any special or noticeable relationship to local small business communities per se, which is why it is counting on outreach partners with whom it has cultivated specific understandings with respect to this particular initiative, as well as press contacts it has nurtured through the years, to help it realize this objective. So while business owners, in their role as individual citizens, may support the organization and its issues, the organization does not have this type of information—what types of jobs individual supporters hold—in its contact database.

Over the past four months, Planet 3000 has managed to reach an agreement with the National Chambers of Commerce to support this particular initiative because the facts indicate a stronger business climate at the local level. And Planet 3000 has continually cultivated members of the business press by holding semiannual briefings for them. It has also spent the past six months identifying and conducting an outreach campaign to local environmental groups and activists who are specifically interested in clean air and transportation issues. By agreeing to provide both national data and local impact information, Planet 3000 has managed to convince at least two groups in each community to take the lead at the local level and participate in this initiative.

Strategy Influences Perceptions.   Because the organization wants to attract small business owners to its cause, it will use strategies that underscore the bottom line. Yet, at the same time, small business owners by definition market their products and services to local consumers, which is why Planet 3000 has formed alliances with local environmental groups who are patrons of the small businesses.

All of the strategies highlight a more rational approach to the issue. In the past, most environmental issues have been framed by the business press either as scientific matters or, when dealing with regulations, as bottom-line matters. In taking its present approach, Planet 3000 hopes to build on the existing perceptions of members of its target audience that this too is a matter of concern regarding the health of their businesses. By relying on the business press, the chambers of commerce, and local reporters to deliver the message, Planet 3000 is helping to ensure that this audience receives this message as a rational, good business sense issue that will help the audience's bottom line grow over time.

Who Controls the Message.   Because the organization is relying heavily on others—whether the press, the chambers of commerce, or local groups—to get the message out, it has to take extra care to make sure that all spokespersons stay on message, reinforcing key points as well as the frame that will most effectively position the issue in the minds of the messengers as the organization wants it framed. Even in the radio actuality and the VNR, where the organization controls the message and the images attached to it, how the recipient of those pieces decides to edit or add will ultimately determine the message received by the primary audience.

The fact that the primary audience will be more receptive to messages delivered by these messengers outweighs the limited control that Planet 3000 will have over how the issue is positioned. The press will lend objectivity through its independent analysis and presentation of the facts, the chambers of commerce will lend credibility to the frame that this is "good for business," and the celebrity will bring a certain glamour to the issue that will rub off on those businesses engaged in the initiative.

The two strategies that will allow the organization to control the message—the engagement packages and the Web site—while reaching the primary audience in its original form, will also be used and modified by the local groups (chambers and environmental activists) in ways that will go beyond the organization's control.

Effort to Implement.   Planet 3000 has spent the past six months building the bridges that are necessary to make these strategies happen. It also has a five-person communications and public affairs staff who can manage and implement all of the strategies. However, during the three months of the initiative's launch, the organization estimates that it will take approximately 60 percent of the staff's time. Once the initiative has taken hold with the local groups—after the first three or four months—the staff time is expected to decrease to about 30 percent. The one outside person the organization will have to bring in is a part-time consultant to do the Web site design and update the site on a regular basis, but the Planet 3000 staff has decided that this is also an opportunity to learn how to manage and update a Web site and expects to take the work in house by the end of the year.

Budget Issues.   Aside from the fax broadcast of the policy analysis and producing the radio actuality, the strategies proposed by the staff are fairly expensive, but the organization sees this stage of the initiative as critical in achieving ultimate success and will continue to raise money for the initiative. The staff expects to keep the costs of the VNR to a minimum by using existing footage from its library and from local sources. It has also negotiated a discounted package deal with the satellite company to transmit the radio actuality and VNR and handle the satellite media tour. The engagement package, while also an expensive proposition, is a key component to ensuring ongoing cooperation and engagement of the national and local chambers of commerce. While the out-of-pocket costs for the Web site are minimal, the fact that an outside consultant will have to be hired to design and produce the site involves a major expense. The poll is also a big-ticket item, but it is serving a dual function for the organization—to help shape more effective messages and strategies for the target audience and to generate interest in the press.

Potential Impact on Other Audiences. All of the strategies will have an impact on multiple audiences because they rely heavily on the press to help distribute the message. Even the engagement packages have press outreach materials for use by the local chambers of commerce. And, while the focus is on local coverage that will influence local audiences, Planet 3000 hopes to tie together the various local coverage and turn the initiative into a regional story it will then build into a national effort. It hopes to time this effort to movement of the legislation through Congress.

Focal Point: The Conference

Whether they are held for the press, affiliates, members, or volunteers, conferences are structured and have a set agenda with one or more speakers—individually or on panels—who present information, after which other attendees—the "listening participants"—are given time to ask questions. This type of conference is often used to raise issues in a way that will grab the attention of or create increased awareness on the part of the "listening participants," who are usually expected to go out and report back on the conference to others (via mass media coverage, internal organizational media, or word of mouth).

The "report back" function is often as important as informing attendees who, at the time, appear to be the primary audience. Because of this, who gets to speak, how strongly the message is framed, and how clearly it is delivered are critical decisions the organization will make, since that ultimately determines the message and the information that those not in attendance eventually receive.

Because the format and structure of a conference is more formal, static, and passive, it is not particularly effective in helping participants work through their beliefs, opinions, values, and attitudes toward an issue, nor is it likely to guarantee that action will be taken. It is, however, an excellent way to build and strengthen relationships with press contacts, members, chapters, affiliates, coalition partners, and the like. More often than not, the formal proceedings are less important to the final impact the conference will have on attendees than the networking and informal conversations that occur.

Focal Point: Radio Actualities

A radio actuality is nothing more than an audio press release. It gives an organization the chance to package news and commentary about a single story, event, or issue in an audio format for distribution to and use by radio stations. A radio actuality has the same elements as the print press release:

- A brief wrap-up that gives the who, what, when, and where of the story
- A sound bite featuring a spokesperson associated with your organization
- A short closing that gives the name and phone number of the media contact at your organization.

The actuality is recorded on an audio cassette that can be either sent directly to radio stations or distributed via a satellite feed as arranged by a number of satellite news services. The stations who decide to use the tape will broadcast it as a complete story (as you've shaped it) or use a part of it (usually the spokesperson's quote). Because of this, your organization's message is likely to remain intact.

Radio actualities are best used when an organization wants to attract coverage by stations in small and/or medium-size markets. Most stations in larger markets do not use radio news feeds; rather, they get their news off syndicated wire services or through their own news operations.

Focal Point: Video News Releases

A video news release (VNR) gives an organization the chance to tell a story in its own words and deliver to the media the images it wants the public to see. A VNR is a short video—from ninety seconds to five minutes—that an organization produces and distributes to local and national media outlets. Often it is used on the local news broadcast, especially in small and medium-size media markets with small news departments. Sometimes only the images are used, with a local newsperson doing the voice-over to the story, using either the script that came with the VNR or a script produced by the news staff. Yet, even when the media don't use actual footage from the VNR, the issue as framed in the VNR often becomes the frame used by the news media to report the story that the VNR is about. This is because, with video, the images tell the story and powerful images can convey a powerful story, even to reporters who may not want to use those exact images on the evening news. Consider the issues that nonprofits tackle and the images that might be associated with those issues:

Clean air	Exhaust fumes, smokestacks, people on oxygen machines
Homelessness	People in the streets digging through trash for food, sleeping on doorways, talking about their experience of getting through the day
Child care	A child walking through a vacant lot alone, a child unlocking the door to an empty house
Poverty	Housing that is crumbling and infested with rats, children playing in litter-strewn streets, the expression of hunger

Organizations interested in producing a VNR should be sure they have a story with news value, effective spokespersons, and compelling visuals. The VNR will include, in the order in which the video is actually put together:

- Credits—the names and titles of featured speakers
- Story summary for news anchor to read to learn what the story is about
- Suggested anchor lead—how you want the local anchorperson to introduce the story
- Tagline—what you want the anchor to say at the end of the story
- The story itself without the sound
- A sound version of the story
- Sound bites—quotes made by speakers other than the reporter, usually accompanied by a "talking head" shot of the person
- B-roll—additional images to illustrate the script

Be truthful and accurate and make the VNR look like the six o'clock news. And use a professional to help you put the VNR together. The cost will be worthwhile in the amount of play the VNR gets. The cost of a VNR will vary considerably depending on a number of factors—from how much production runs to how many outlets you want to reach. The average cost, for planning purposes, ranges from $3,000 to $25,000.

Focal Point: Satellite Media Tours

A tool used by national, regional, or state groups to reach local broadcast news media without having to travel, the satellite media tour is just that: it allows an organization's spokesperson or another expert whom the organization wishes to get on local news broadcasts to be interviewed by local newspersons—usually the local anchorperson of the evening news. While the technology is most often used by national news shows—like *Nightline* and *The Newshour with Jim Lehrer*—when they want to interview one or several guests who are in a different city than where the broadcast is originating, it is also available to organizations who want to tell their stories to people through local channels, as opposed to national channels, whose attention may be more difficult to grab. Satellite media tours are also used in addition to national coverage of an issue, expanding the exposure of the organization's spokesperson as well as of the issue.

The outreach to local news producers is usually handled by the organization's staff or a consultant working for the group. The issue the spokesperson talks about is pitched as any news story would be to any reporter. If it is a national issue, the staff member should try to localize the problem so that it's easy for the producer to see why he or she should make time for the interview on the evening news. Interviews are scheduled on the same day within a set timeframe—for example, from 1:00 to 4:00 eastern time. The organization books the time with a company that has a facility to handle the live production (which entails a two-way voice hookup and a two-way video feed so that the individuals can see each other on the studio monitor). The interview is recorded at both ends—the production facility and the local broadcast station—usually for broadcast on the evening news.

Focal Point: Why Use the World Wide Web

The World Wide Web is the multimedia information delivery system of the Internet. It works on the premise that information can be layered or "tiered" so that it is delivered to the recipient in more manageable chunks that can either stand alone or lead to more information (for more information on tiered information systems, see Appendix C.) Through the use of words, graphics, sound, and video, organizations can create a more interactive experience. People use the Web to do research and retrieve information as well as to publish information for others to look at. In order to access the Web, a person needs a computer, a browser (which is a type of software program), access to an Internet account through an Internet service provider (often called an ISP), a modem, and a telephone line (in some cases, the local cable system can provide a hookup).

While colorful images dancing on a screen, audio programs providing the latest news (using Real Audio[2] software), and the ability to jump from one point to another as one's interest is piqued can be very enticing and engrossing, many visitors still lack high-speed access (via a high-speed modem, ISDN, T1 or T3 lines, or cable) to the World Wide Web. What this means is that the transfer of information and images takes time—sometimes 20 to 30 seconds, which is a lot when you're staring at a screen. If an organization doesn't plan for this, it will lose many interested visitors.

To visit a Web site, the user opens the Web browser and types in the Web site address. As with a book, the first page a visitor sees is the cover— the home page. The home page contains key words, icons, or images a visitor can click on not only to access any of the other pages on the site, but eventually to end up on other organizations' sites. This "linking" makes the Web a layered resource with literally a world of information at the user's fingertips.

Organizations create Web sites for a variety of reasons: to provide instant information about programs or issues, to sign up volunteers or activists, to educate visitors through interactive programming, to attract attention for an initiative or campaign, to poll their members or other constituencies, or to provide affiliated organizations with graphically designed electronic files of information that can be used in publications produced by those organizations. By linking Web sites of many organizations involved in an issue, the technology can create a clearinghouse of information that not only introduces visitors to the many groups involved in the issue but also provides access to information on those groups (in addition to information on the issue).

The other way nonprofit organizations use the World Wide Web is to do research. This is usually done through a number of search engines that can be accessed at no charge via the browser, by clicking on the search button. The

---

[2] Most Web sites that offer an audio portion or program provide visitors with the capacity to download the receiver part of the RealAudio software free of charge. It is built into newer versions of browsers.

trick is to know how to narrow down a description of your search so that you don't end up getting citations to 10,000 articles to review. Most browsers offer users tips on how to get the most out of a search. Yet many proprietary databases don't allow access through the Internet. Anyone doing serious research would do well to include a trip to the library as well as a visit to the Web to gather data. Furthermore, when doing research on the Web, make sure that the source is reputable. There is no guarantee of quality information on the Web—although quality information definitely exists—so anyone using the Web to do research should confirm that the source and the material are in fact legitimate.

Focal Point: Delivery and Distribution Messages

How something is delivered conveys a message in and of itself—for example, how urgent this information is, how important this message is (how much the organization paid to get it to me), how unique it is to my concerns.

1. *Bulk mail:* We're drowning in it—from bills to fund-raising letters to newsletters to catalogs. Even when it is differentiated by virtue of the fact that the recipient truly supports your organization and looks forward to reading about your organization and its issues, bulk mail in and of itself sends a signal that "this piece has been distributed widely." Even when letters are "personalized," the recipient knows the message is generic—not specifically tailored to the reader and his or her individual concerns.

2. *Postal mail—first class:* Invitations, personal and professional correspondence, thank-you notes, birthday cards—first-class mail signals that this is a message specifically created for the recipient. It does not necessarily convey urgency, but rather importance and a higher relatedness of the subject matter to the recipient.

3. *Overnight delivery or messenger:* This type of special delivery instantly confers importance and urgency on the material. The recipient knows that a premium price was paid to deliver the message and that this type of handling often transfers specialness or exclusivity to the message itself.

4. *Fax:* Although this is an immediate delivery of print material from the sender to the recipient, it has also become more commonplace, so that it no longer conveys the same sense of urgency it used to.

Another characteristic of fax delivery is that there is usually a prior relationship between the sender and the recipient. Even a broadcast fax—which might be similar to bulk mail in that the message is not "unique" to the recipient—has probably been agreed to or "authorized" by the recipient beforehand.

5. *Handouts:* This delivery method conveys the most immediacy because it involves human intervention. Whether it is an exercise passed out at a workshop or a leaflet handed out in a shopping mall, the human interaction usually will ensure that the piece gets looked at—although not necessarily read! Thus, the urgency of the message will rely heavily on the context in which the print piece is handed out—for example, how well you've targeted your audience (have you gone to the place where your target audience is?), how relevant the topic is to the recipients, and how successfully the piece has utilized the attention-getting components outlined previously.

FINDING WHAT WORKS FOR YOUR ORGANIZATION

There are many variables to consider when deciding on which strategies should go into your plan and which can be deleted without pulling down the whole effort; it is not an easy task. Finding a strategy may be a matter of trial and error no matter how much analysis went into the decision making; how well the strategy is implemented also comes into play. That is why, when an organization decides to implement strategies with which it has no experience, it is a good idea to bring in an expert at least the first time around. If such is the case, find someone who will be willing to take the time to teach staff members the steps involved so that next time the staff may be in a better position to carry out the strategy by themselves or, at the very least, with less outside help.

Appropriate strategies and vehicles are a key component to the communications plan. They deliver the message and play a critical role in how your audience will negotiate that message.

CH0402.DOC
Exercise #7: Identify strategies to reach your target audiences. There are many communications strategies that can be and have been used to achieve an organization's objectives, too many to suggest here as new ones are created nearly every day to respond

to new challenges that organizations face. At this stage of the planning process, brainstorm and list as many ideas as you and others working with you can generate before deciding which ones will withstand the final cut that will be made in Chapter 5, using the criteria outlined in the worksheet to help you make those decisions.

CH0401.DOC

WORKSHEETS FOR STEP #4

Audience Groups

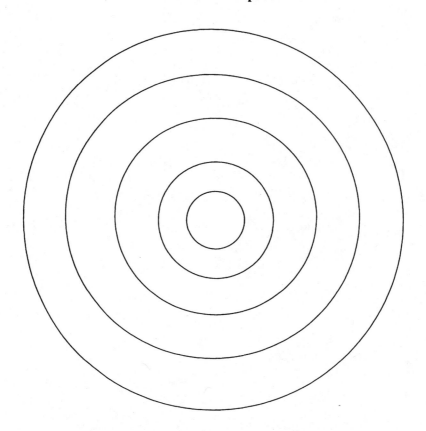

CH0402.DOC

Objective: _____
Target Audience: _____

Possible Strategies	Doable	Responsive to audience	Appropriate to relationship	Affordable
#1: _____	☐	☐	☐	☐

How will this strategy affect the message? | How will it affect the audience's perception? _____

Will it have a positive, negative, or neutral impact on other audiences?   ☐ Positive   ☐ Negative   ☐ Neutral

Possible Strategies	Doable	Responsive to audience	Appropriate to relationship	Affordable
#2: _____	☐	☐	☐	☐

How will this strategy affect the message? | How will it affect the audience's perception? _____

Will it have a positive, negative, or neutral impact on other audiences?   ☐ Positive   ☐ Negative   ☐ Neutral

(Continued)

Rating scale	1	2	3	4	5
Responsive to audience	Highly responsive				Unresponsive
Appropriate to relationship	Very appropriate				Inappropriate
Strategy affects perception	Emotional				Rational
Strategy affects message	Most control over message				Least control
Strategy affects message	Most control over interpretation				Least control
Effort to implement	Least				Most
Cost to implement	Least expensive				Most expensive
Impact on others	Impact on others				No impact

Strategy	Responsiveness	Relationship	Perception (rational=5)	Message control	Interpretation control	Effort to implement	Cost	Impact on others	Totals
What the score means									

Given the above, rank the strategies from most important to least important

1
2
3
4
5
6
7
8

Step #5:
When and Where?

Build a Plan, Create a Calendar

Now that all the research, analysis, and brainstorming has been done, it's time to bring all the pieces together and build the communications plan. All the possible strategies that have been considered will now be sorted through and prioritized. By bringing together all these strands—which strategies to implement, when each will happen, what it will take to make each happen, and who will be responsible for various tasks, strategies, and objectives—you will create a road map for your organization's communications. Although everyone's plans will look different on paper—some people prefer text, while others prefer charts and lists—the plan will include the following components listed in Exhibit 5-1. Items 1 through 7 have been discussed and completed during the exercises in the previous chapters. In this chapter, we pick up with item 8 to create a plan from which your organization can work.

THE WHEN AND WHERE

Having brainstormed possible strategies and vehicles for each audience and having prioritized them based on the various criteria set out in the previous chapter, you now must think through the "where and when" of the plan. The

Exhibit 5-1   The Planning Process

1. A situational analysis—internal and external—within which your organization is working, including how the media is framing the issues with which your organization is concerned

2. Your organizational goal(s)

3. Each goal's program objectives

4. Communications objectives for each program objective

5. Audiences (prioritized from most important to least important) for each communications objective and an analysis of their perspectives, lifestyles, priorities, values, and so on

6. Targeted messages for each objective, modified for each audience

7. The strategies you've decided on for each audience and specific vehicles that will be needed to implement those strategies

8. A timeline/task list for each vehicle with individuals responsible for each task and strategy

9. An estimated budget and where financial resources will come from (reallocation, new funding, in-kind contributions)

10. A calendar of organizational activities (already planned), national, state, and local events or holidays, activities other organizations are planning that have a connection to your organization's program and/or issues, and so forth, to help you manage your plan

strategies your organization decides to pursue must be organized in a way that will fulfill your communications objectives and create new momentum for your issues, your organization's programs, and so on, while at the same time responding to existing organizational activities and external events. Think of it as a cascade of actions that keeps moving your organization and its audiences toward the realization of your program goals. Your plan will spell out, one day at a time, the communications route your organization needs to follow. The plan, while set on paper, will be a "living" document in that it changes and grows, always responding to new opportunities, new challenges, and new options.

PUTTING IT ALL TOGETHER

Begin by taking a calendar that tracks organizational and other relevant external activities, holidays, commemorative events, and the like. On this calendar, note communications projects already in the works.

Next to the calendar, place your planning sheet for your first communications objective's top-priority audience. In addition to the objective clearly stated, this planning sheet should include what you know (or need to find out) about this audience, targeted messages (tested or untested), and a prioritized list of strategies and/or vehicles to move this audience toward your objective(s).

Select "target dates" for each strategy. These are the dates on which the audience will experience or receive the communication. A simple example is a quarterly mailing. You would note not only the date of the mailing, but also, more importantly, the estimated time for the mailing to land. The same would be true for a fax broadcast, an e-mail alert, even a press release. Note that when your target audience is an "outreach partner"—like the press, legislative staff, and so on—when they experience the communication will be the first target date, with the second target date noted as the approximate time the story might be expected to run.

These target dates will be used to judge when a follow-up or another new communication with that audience should take place—later that week, next week, next month, and so forth. By tracking these target dates you will get a clear picture of the frequency of your organization's communication with that audience and be in a better position to assess how often the audience has been exposed to the issue as well as to your message. Chapter 7 discusses evaluating the quality of the communication and its impact as well as how to make use of that information.

As the various strategies come together for a single audience group, consider the following:

- How will this "schedule" of communications feel to your target audience?

- Will audience members experience it as a continuum or as scattershot?

- Looked at over time as a whole, will these efforts create the necessary momentum and gradually get the individuals within the target group to do what you need them to do in order to achieve your objective?

Once the strategies are on paper with appropriate target dates set on the calendar, work backward to fill in the various tasks that must be done in order to successfully implement each strategy. For example, if a monthly newsletter is a strategy your organization wants to use to keep its volunteers informed, the various tasks involved—writing and researching the articles, gathering photos and graphics, layout, proofreading, printing, getting the mailing list to the mail house, and so on—must all be plotted out on a time-line with the appropriate person's name and an estimated time for how long each step will take in order to get the newsletter into the volunteers' hands on the target date.

While a newsletter is a relatively simple, straightforward strategy, even the most complex communications campaign can and must be broken down into its component parts before it can be implemented, managed, and changed as the need arises.

After you've plotted out six months for a single audience group, go through the same process with the second audience group, then the third. Detail each step and mark the dates on your calendar. This will help you decide on your organization's "breaking point" or "communications toler-ance level." In addition, by "slicing and dicing" the timeline, you can pull together detailed staff and volunteer task lists with deadlines and deliver-ables for which they are responsible. The manager of the communications plan can use these tools to ensure that all the work is done in a timely fashion. Here are some issues to keep in mind as you begin creating your work plan.

Guiding Questions

- What is actually doable?
- Does one strategy serve multiple audiences?
- Are we maximizing the impact of what we plan to do by coordinating adequate follow-up?
- Is the combination of all these strategies affordable?
- Is the time available to do everything realistic?
- Do we have the staff expertise to handle this or will we need to bring someone in to help us out?
- Do various strategies work together for more than one audience group?
- Do they overlap unnecessarily?
- Can two or more strategies be combined without adversely impacting on various audience groups?
- Do any of the messages or strategies contradict or hinder each other?
- If we can't do it all, which strategies can we cut and still reach our objective?

CASE STUDY: PLANET 3000

Author's note: Although an organization would have more than a single program goal and objective, this case study is meant to be illustrative only. Thus, various components are only suggested and not fully fleshed out in order to simplify the process and highlight the necessary steps.

The Situational Analysis[1]

Publics That May Be Connected to Your Organization			
			1 = truly competitive 2 = somewhat competitive in these areas 3 = not really competitive
Category/name	*For/ against*	*Reason for connection/ stake in organization*	*Competitive status*

Place a check in front of those organizations with whom your organization might collaborate

Colleagues at other organizations

☑ John Raym	Ⓕ A	Executive director of environmental coalition	1 2③
☑ Pamela Scholler	Ⓕ A	Leading researcher of ecosystems	①2 3
☑ Michael Estes	Ⓕ A	Program officer of our largest funder	1 2③

Organizations with similar program interests and values

☑ Environmental working group	Ⓕ A	Environmental policy research + education	1 2③
☑ Ecotrust	Ⓕ A	Conservation + new economic models + ecosystems	1②3
☑ The National Aububon Society	Ⓕ A	Conserve/restore ecosystems = well-being of human civilization	1②3
❑ Natural Resources Defense Council	Ⓕ A	"Stewardship of the earth"	1 2③
☑ The Nature Conservancy	Ⓕ A	Protection of ecosystems/resource management	1 2③

Organizations that oppose our work

❑ Lambda Alpha International	F Ⓐ	Land economics researchers	①2 3
❑ American Land Rights Association	F Ⓐ	Wise use—people first and only	1 2③

(Continued)

[1] This situational analysis is an example of the types of information that would be included and why such information would be important to know. While some of the organizations mentioned are real, others are fictional, as are the names of individuals and their affiliations. Likewise, information having to do with demographic, economic, political, social, and technological trends as well as the national media highlights is fictitious and for illustration purposes only.

Category/name	For/ against	Reason for connection/ stake in organization	Competitive status
❑ National Center for Public Policy Research	F (A)	Wise use research group	(1) 2 3
❑ Center for Defense of Free Enterprise	F (A)	Wise use advocacy and education	1 2 (3)
❑ Activists/advocates	(F) A	Care about environment/understand importance of ecosystems and believe human systems can change	
❑ Board members	(F) A	Committed to organization's mission 100%	
Private foundations			
❑ Pew Charitable Trusts	(F) A	Cares about ecosystems; needs to see connection to human systems development	
❑ W. Alton Jones Foundation	(F) A	Understands connection of ecological to human systems	
❑ Joyce Mertz-Gilmore Foundation	(F) A	Cares about ecosystems; needs to see connection to human systems development	
☑ Turner Foundation	(F) A	Understands connection of ecological to human systems	
Corporate foundations			
❑ AMR/American	(F) A	Environmental support (board connection)	
❑ Gannett	(F) A	Supports public education on environment	
❑ Donors	(F) A	75% have at least 3-year history	
❑ Community leaders	F A	Majority view ecosystems as irrelevant to their communities	
Community groups/local environmental groups *(target 6 communities in 6 regions—partners for town meetings)*			
☑ Madison in the Balance	(F) A	Studies ecosystems in Midwest	1 2 (3)
☑ Life and Harmony in Phoenix	(F) A	More focused on pollution/ population; needs to see connection to ecosystems	1 2 (3)
☑ Baltimore Eco-more	(F) A	Studies ecosystems in MD/DE/DC	1 2 (3)
☑ Boston in Balance	(F) A	Research and advocacy for NE ecosystems (Partners with Harvard)	1 2 (3)
☑ South Florida Lives	(F) A	New group; focused on restoring ecosystems	1 2 (3)

(Continued)

Category/name	For/ against	Reason for connection/ stake in organization	Competitive status
☑ Iowans for the Earth	(F) A	Working to reestablish prairies	1 2 (3)
☐ Organized religious groups	F (A)	Against evolutionary theory—humans do God's work	
Reporters, editors			
☐ Tom Abrams, NY Times	F A	Scientist—understands ecosystems; challenges connection to possible human systems	
☐ Regina Elderson, Washington Post	F A	Political reporter—likes the concept	
☐ Ronnie Langley, Newsweek	F A	Good on environmental issues; hasn't connected to need for human systems to change	
☐ Jonathan Orris, US News & World Report	F A	Subscribes to free-market approach	
Government officials/policy makers			
☐ Ellis McGill, EPA Chief	F A	We're one of many voices in the mix	
☐ Joanna Shatzkin, Secretary of Interior	F A	Need to get ecosystems on radar screen	
☐ Sarah Jonis, Chief, National Economic Council	F A	Seems interested in theory; not sure about accepting practical implication tests	
☐ Parents	F A	Strongly representative of donor/ activist base	
☑ Educators/teachers	F A	Use organization's curriculum materials	
Business—corporations, associations, leaders			
☑ Able Technology	(F) A	Researching ecosystem laws for ideas for new products and processes	
☐ Wainwright Industries	F (A)	Southwest mining; support wise use	
☑ National Chambers of Commerce	(F) A	Interested in pilot test with select members	
☐ Children and youth	F A	Planet 3000's next generation program	
☐ Health care providers	F A	Healthy Planet, Healthy Lives program	
Others			
☑ Researchers and academics (allied theories)	(F) A	Use their work; need participation/ leadership	1 2 3
☐ Researchers and academics (wise use theories)	F (A)	They pose strong argument to issue	1 2 3
☐ Researchers and academics (neutral/undecided)	F A	They're critical in validating theory	1 2 3

Somewhat Competitive Organizations

Ecotrust. Researches conservation measures (conserving ecosystems) and looking at ways to develop new economic models that are in harmony with those ecosystems. We take the next step, arguing that ecosystems could teach us how to invent new cultural and economic systems. Would make good partner.

The National Aububon Society. Researches and actively works to restore ecosystems and believes that the well-being of human civilization relies on healthy ecosystems. Again, we take it the next step by positing that human civilization is simply another ecosystem that is out of balance and can be restored to balance by taking lessons from "natural" laws. Possible partner.

The External Environment

Demographics. Has there been a shift or change in the populations or the makeup of the communities you serve?
    While there are obvious demographic shifts happening in the country and the world, this doesn't seem to be impacting our work or our immediate plans for the future either positively or negatively. However, this year we hope to study whether parents of children who have had exposure to environmental science curricula are becoming more aware of eco-human system concepts. Our hope is that the boomers, who helped launch the first Earth Day and were at the forefront of the environmental movement, will be reinvigorated as their children move into junior high.

Economics. How do donors perceive the economy and what does that mean for our financial well-being? How will the economy impact the amount of funds available from private foundations this year? Is the economy shifting in ways that will cause a demand in services from the populations we serve? Is the economy such that there will be a decline in the populations we serve? What about unemployment?
    The economy is steady with low unemployment, which creates a more open climate for new ideas and new money. Because of this, people seem to be more concerned with quality of life issues, which we've seen work for us in the past. While we don't view our work as a quality of life concern, the fact is that the vast majority of people need to feel secure before they will venture off into an area that clearly has to do with conceptualizing change. Although we don't expect to gain a large number of new donors, we are targeting small

to medium-size donors and expect that the strong economy will translate into at least an 8 to 12 percent growth in our donor base.

Technological Developments.   What are the latest trends in business technology? How might we use these to become more cost-effective? To reach a larger population? What are the latest products or trends in technology having to do with the programs or issues our organization is interested in—health delivery, social services, job training, education, and so on? How will these trends impact our organization and its business? Can we afford to apply this technology to create a better product, provide more effective services, become more economically stable?

We're keeping an eye on the progress of electronic fund transfers so that we can take advantage of this to raise funds on the Internet. It isn't quite there yet, and even when the technology is ready, it will probably still take a few years until people feel comfortable using it on a broad basis. We also hope to use videoconferencing and satellite hookups this year to experiment with linking communities we're working in so that they can share experiences across the miles in a more interactive way. And, a team of our researchers is working with several outside experts on a CD-ROM simulation that allows individuals to simulate what happens when specific ecosystem principles are introduced into a variety of human systems. Ideally, we hope to be able to market this as a commercial educational product, much like SimCity 2000—using it as a way to reach people who otherwise might not be engaged by other types of communication on these issues.

Political.   What is the national, local, and state political forecast for the next six months? Is there anything that affects our organization—either programmatically or functionally—on the "radar screen"? If the winds blow our way, what can we expect? If they go against us, what's the worst that can happen? Are there hints of something that we're not seeing?

While the national administration is relatively friendly to environmentalists at the moment, it is still driven by economic concerns. We hope that our pilot projects in the six communities—with the communities themselves recommending policy changes—will result in the beginning of a shift in policy, getting the first of these recommendations onto the radar screen in two more years. Next year is an election year, so this may change. The environmental coalition will be working to hold its own. We plan on working at the local level with our partner communities to ensure that environmental health stays on the agenda. Hopefully, our town hall meetings will be the foundation on which to build that visibility.

Social.   What social or cultural trends are we seeing in the community, in the state, in the nation? What does this mean for our organization and its work? What social or cultural values do our constituents subscribe to? Have these values changed recently? If so, why? What does it mean in our relationship to our constituency? What is the mood of the nation? Our community? What's the latest fear in society? What's the latest demand?

We're told that the mood of the country is positive on environmental issues with an underlying, unspoken fear of what will happen to the planet in the future. While people seem intrigued by "natural laws," they also don't recognize their own connection to these laws. Society does not seem connected to nature. That is perhaps our biggest challenge. While our staff prefers a positive approach to the issue, we are cognizant of the fact that fear drives the public agenda and the public's attention. And, while specific environmental problems—clean air, global warming—do claim sporadic attention, society has a hard time seeing the intrinsic connections that lie below the individual problems, making what we do that much more challenging.

Current Positioning of Issue(s) in the Mass Media (Highlights from Longer Framing Memo).   When ecosystems are covered in the media, it is as an "other"—something out there that we, as humans who are in control of the earth, must save. This victimization of ecosystems, while, to some degree true due to the path of human civilization, is not the best frame for our work and our objectives. It glorifies the status quo while keeping the ecosystems separate and, to a certain degree mysterious, which only reinforces the "otherness" we must eliminate if we are to convince communities that they will gain, rather than lose, something by modeling their systems on ecosystems.

Organizational Culture.   Planet 3000 is very experimental and isn't afraid to "go out on a limb" preferably with research that substantiates our theories. But, since we are trying to find new ways of combining human systems and the principles of ecosystems, we have to be willing to offer "radical" theories for discussion.

Our staff is committed and has autonomy in the day-to-day flow of business. However, any position a staff member is advocating has to be reviewed and "vetted" by a staff team that challenges the proposed theory or concept before it makes its way to the world at large. This approach has worked to foster creative thought as well as teamwork without the resentment that might occur from a "top-down" approach. Instead there is a feeling that ideas are "bouncing off the walls." The majority of the staff members understand that we will only move the issue forward if everyone shares knowledge. In fact, this understanding is one of the things human resources asks about in job interviews.

The Board has expressed a desire to specifically partner with local and regional environmental groups to get the "eco-human systems" theory on their radar screens and into local programs.

Program Objectives. Given that the organization is in the middle of a five-year plan, our growth has been fairly well plotted out and what we hope to accomplish appears doable. This is a consensus of the president, board, and department directors. Our objectives do address the needs of the external environment in that we are relying heavily on building research support for our theories while interesting local communities in the "natural order" and how it translates into everyday living. We see the two sides as having equal priority, because the community activists can inform the researchers as to what problems they're facing, and the researchers can then attempt to structure research around those problems.

Management Objectives. Every month there is a full staff meeting, at which time program and management (cost efficiency and team-building efforts) are reviewed with an open discussion of problems that staff members experience in their daily routines. The director of operations and the director of evaluation are responsible for this effort and regularly update guidelines, incorporating information from these meetings.

Human Resources. Last year we strengthened our grassroots organizing/local outreach staff to complement our research staff, which has been growing at a fairly even pace. Members of our research staff not only work with each other but partner with outside researchers at academic centers in an effort to leverage our human resources. We have found that this approach has the added result of bringing outside researchers into our camp, and they more actively support our programs. We currently have on staff three world-renowned researchers who have helped us get the attention of the press and policy makers while generating respect for our work in the larger research community.

Due to expansion, we need to increase the operations/administrative staff this year as our systems and the need of program people for more general support have grown along with the program. There is a consensus that this type of help would cut back on the amount of overtime program staff currently puts in.

Our goal this year is to grow our advocate base by approximately 6000 to 9000 contacts in the cities we've targeted as possible future sites for pilot programs. It is critical that we get this type of support in order to expect any sort of pilot program launch in the future.

Financial Resources.   We've met our budgets over the past three years and expect to be in the black at the end of this year. While we have not been able to set up a reserve fund, we have managed to garner consistent support from a core of donors and a select group of private foundations.

We've put an interdisciplinary team in place at Planet 3000 to look at ways our information products might generate revenue for the organization. We've learned quite a bit about this over the past two years in marketing and selling our school curriculum; we hope to apply this newfound knowledge to other program areas.

Physical Infrastructure.   Due to our growth in the past two years, we've had to reconfigure our space and eventually we will need approximately 3000 additional square feet in the main office. While current space is conducive to our team approach, there is the sense that more private space would be useful, especially for researchers. We are solving this problem by asking people to telecommute on an as-needed basis, which seems to be a temporary fix at best. While this won't be a crisis for another eighteen months, we need to begin figuring out long-term solutions by the end of the year. If possible, we would like to stay in the neighborhood—where staff feels comfortable and safe, and where we are close to the main library for research needs—but we may have to consider moving to another space in the neighborhood if we can't reconfigure yet again. If we do decide that moving is the only approach left to us, we plan to have a consultant talk to individual staff members to prioritize our most important considerations regarding a new space.

Technological Infrastructure.   Our computer infrastructure is healthy, although not cutting-edge. While we have a LAN that provides connectivity within the organization as well as internal and external e-mail, not everyone has direct access to the Internet from his or her desktop. This year's project is to make that access happen and operations is looking into the most cost-effective way that will not create a bottleneck as demand heightens for both research work and organizing. As part of this project, we expect to add the capacity for individuals to fax directly from their desktops to minimize tie-ups at the fax machine.

The organizing team is also about halfway done with having their advocate database programmed and plan to work in tandem with several of the researchers to put together a survey to assess local attitudes toward the eco-human system concept in our six target markets. We plan to bring in a trainer for two days to give everyone in the organizing department training on the database so that they can use it to its full capacity.

Our phone system, which was installed three years ago with voice mail, is still adequate since data lines are put in as they are needed. Operations expects that our system will continue to be sufficient once the data lines are returned to voice use (when Internet access is handled through a separate T1 line). We've also hired a part-time receptionist to take calls from 10:00 to 3:00. In monitoring the general voice mailbox, we found that most of the calls come in during that time, so we've decided it would be more cost-efficient to have someone there to answer those calls immediately than to have to pass messages on only to return calls and have staff spend time playing phone tag.

How will this information help or hinder us in the year ahead? We are not stepping into this year wearing rose-colored glasses. There are a lot of things on our plate, yet, given the above realities, they are all doable. The demographic and economic climates appear to be working in our favor, while the social and political climates are not harming or helping us in any particular way at the moment, paving the way for our plan to unfold in a nonhostile climate.

This may also be a good time to launch our researcher outreach, given the increased recognition of the need to save ecosystems. The soil seems fertile to begin suggesting the eco-human systems principles to these experts as the next area of research. Our connections with outside researchers are good and we have worked to build links with other environmental organizations.

Mission Statement

Planet 3000 is committed to healing the earth. Using its research into how natural ecosystems work, Planet 3000 develops policy recommendations and pilot projects that apply these underlying principles to human ecosystems such as cultural habits, social structures, commercial ventures, and the like. It advocates for the establishment of human ecosystems that are in harmony with life on the planet. When the human social order is brought back into balance with life on earth, diversity of all living things can be sustained and the evolutionary process that has guided and nurtured life on the planet for millions of years can continue unabated.

Dates of Important Events/Activities

January	1	New Year's Day
	15	Martin Luther King Jr.'s Birthday
February	2	Groundhog Day
	12	Lincoln's Birthday
	14	Valentine's Day
	16	Presidents' Day
	22	Washington's Birthday
March	17	St. Patrick's Day
April	1	April Fools' Day
	11	Passover
	12	Easter
	22	**Earth Day**
May	10	Mother's Day
	25	Memorial Day
June	14	Flag Day
	21	Father's Day

Communications Plan from January 1 through June 30

Program Goal #1:
To research, document, and explain the connection between the food supply and population growth in nonhuman and human ecosystems.

Measurable Objective A–Goal #1:
By July 1, to conduct a literature review on research done over the past fifteen years as well as on current/ongoing research projects and their hypotheses in order to categorize various theories into a few overarching principles.

Communications Objective (Building Awareness/Relationship Building):
To build awareness for Planet 3000, this research project, and its findings among 100 key researchers who've done work in this area so that they will

publicly endorse our work and our findings (see Exhibits 5-2 and 5-3 for a task list and calendar timetable).

Target Audience:
Individuals who have done research in the area of ecosystems and human population and agricultural trends or on tribal ecosystems.

Message:
As a leading researcher, you understand the balance that exists in healthy ecosystems. We are bringing together people like you to look at how natural laws can be applied to human systems. By creating a web of information based on the web of life, we can figure out how these laws can be used to bring the earth back into balance.

Strategies:
1. Develop a contact database of key researchers, noting their principal theses.

2. Conduct and moderate an online forum, posting summaries of different research studies periodically during the literature review to stimulate discussion.

3. Send announcements to academic reviews and journals about the project and how readers can join the online forum.

4. Meet with researchers from environmental groups working in this area.

5. Fax broadcast a research update on a monthly basis to our contact list, highlighting groups of studies as they are analyzed and categorized into an overarching principle; note where the full text of the research report can be found.

6. Hold an audio press conference for science reporters with key experts to answer specific questions. Arrange for local activists to be available to speak about the human interest side of the story.

Vehicles to Be Developed and Produced:
1. Listserv (online forum)

2. Press announcements

3. Fact sheet on Planet 3000

4. Purpose statement and work plan for research project

5. Biographical statement of project director

6. Research update

Exhibit 5-2   Overall Responsibility for Communications Objective #1A:
Jan Howard
Total Out of Pocket: $9155

Strategy/task	Target date	Person responsible	Cost
1. Database	**1 Mar**	**Lilly**	
Set up/program database	25 Jan	Mark P. (consultant)	$1200
Research contact info, theses	15 Feb	Jan	
Input data, run reports	25 Feb	Lilly	
2. Online forum	**20 Mar**	**Jan**	
Set up listserv with Internet service provider	1 Mar	Lilly	$ 100
Write welcome message, forum announcement, invitation to join	5 Mar	Sam	
Set up e-mail distribution list for invitation	10 Mar	Lilly	
Send out announcement to list	15 Mar	Lilly	
Post first message	15 Mar	Jan	
Post follow-up messages	Every other day	Jan	
3. Press release to journals	**1 Feb**	**Sam**	
	For spring issues		
Write press release, fact sheet	25 Jan	Sam	
Set up fax broadcast list— 100 reporters	22 Jan	Lilly	
Send release as fax broadcast	31 Jan	Lilly	$ 25
Select follow-up phone calls	1 Feb	Sam	
4. Meetings with researchers	**20 Feb & 25 Apr**	**Jan**	
Reserve meeting space, refreshments	3 Jan	Lilly	$4800
Write invitations	3 Jan	Sam	
Collect/input contact information	3 Jan	Lilly	
Write purpose, work plan, agenda	3 Jan	Jan	
Print envelopes, copy, mail invitations	4 Jan	Lilly	$ 20
Follow-up phone calls to confirm	25 Jan & 16 Apr	Lilly	
Copy, collate information packets	25 Jan & 16 Apr	Lilly	$ 80
Name tags, participant list	31 Jan & 20 Apr	Lilly	$ 10
Reminder of second meeting written, sent	15 Mar	Lilly	$ 20
Draft preliminary research report	1 Apr	Jan	
Draft highlights of report	3 Apr	Sam	
Copy and mail report	4 Apr	Lilly	$ 100

(Continued)

Exhibit 5-2 *(Continued)*

Strategy/task	Target date	Person responsible	Cost
Invite two reporters, exclusive— second meeting	12 Apr	Sam	
Rent two laptops to document sessions		Lilly & Sam	$1000
5. Research update (begin March)	**15th of each month**	**Sam**	
Draft monthly updates	5th of each month	Sam	
Review/edit monthly updates	10th of each month	Jan	
Fax broadcast updates (500 researchers)	15th of each month	Lilly	$1800

Communications Objective (Engagement/Working Through):
To engage two dozen key researchers from a variety of disciplines in the process of conceptualizing how these theories could apply to or influence social structures and our cultural order as well as economic matters.

Target Audience:

- Key researchers from cultural anthropology, ecology, biology, economics, and systems design
- Environmental advocacy and research organizations

Message:
Ecosystems use checks and balances to nurture life on the planet. As humans, we live under a second set of laws, creating conflict and disrupting diversity. Help create new theories based on natural law to guide modern society toward a future that is in harmony with the rest of life.

Strategies:

1. Recruit an advisory committee of five critically acclaimed researchers to lend their names and stature to launching this effort.

2. Recruit at least three other organizational sponsors (from allies) and convene two 3-day invitation-only summit meetings; document all sessions.

3. Create visual maps that illustrate how each theory or principle works and what impact it has on individual populations within the ecosystem, with an accompanying analogy to modern culture.

Exhibit 5-3   Communications Calendar

January	3	Reserve meeting space, refreshments	Lilly
		Write researcher invitations	Sam
		Collect/input researcher contact info	Lilly
		Write purpose, work plan, agenda	Jan
	4	Print envelopes, copy, mail invitations	Lilly
	6	Action Team meeting	
	19	Martin Luther King Jr. Day (observed)	
	20	Action Team meeting	
	22	Set up fax broadcast list (reporters)	Lilly
	25	Set up database	Mark P.
		Write press release, fact sheet	Sam
		Phone calls to confirm researchers	Lilly
		Copy/collate info packets for researchers	Lilly
	31	**Fax broadcast press release**	Lilly
		Print name tags, participant list	Lilly
February	1	Follow-up phone calls to journals	Sam
	2	Groundhog Day	
	3	Action Team meeting	
	12	Lincoln's Birthday	
	14	Valentine's Day	
	15	Collect researcher contact info and theses	Jan
	17	Action Team meeting	
	20	**First researcher meeting**	
	22	Washington's Birthday	
	25	Input data, run contact list, proofread	Lilly
March	1	**Researcher contact database operational**	
		Set up listserv	Lilly
	3	Action Team meeting	
	5	Write listserv welcome message, forum announcement, invitation to join	Sam
		Draft March research update	Sam
	10	Review/edit March research update	Jan
		Set up e-mail distribution list for researchers	Lilly
	15	Send out e-mail listserv announcement	Lilly
		Post first message to listserv	Jan
		Write and send reminder of second researcher meeting	Lilly
		Fax broadcast research update	Lilly
	17	Post follow-up listserv message	Jan
		Action Team meeting	
	19	Post follow-up listserv message	Jan
	21	Post follow-up listserv message	Jan
		First Day of Spring	
	23	Post follow-up listserv message	Jan
	25	Post follow-up listserv message	Jan
	27	Post follow-up listserv message	Jan
	29	Post follow-up listserv message	Jan
	31	Post follow-up listserv message	Jan

4. Conduct a private listserv for invitees to continue their thinking via e-mail.

5. Create written summaries in nonacademic language of various proposals or theories that result from the summit; circulate the summaries for comments.

Vehicles to Be Produced:

1. Stationery for the project featuring advisory committee members

2. Background materials for each summit meeting

3. Name tags

4. Summit attendee lists

5. Audio documentation for all summit sessions

6. Visual maps with written impact/analogy summaries

7. Listserv

8. Nonacademic written summaries of proposals to be used to develop pilot projects testing ecosystem principles on human ecosystem(s)

Measurable Objective B–Goal #1, Which Is Also a Communications Objective (Building Awareness/Engaging the Audience to Work Through):
To educate community leaders and youth in six communities about different ecosystem principles in order to help them reach consensus and articulate possible public policy recommendations during the next eighteen months.

Communications Objective (Relationship Building/ Moving the Audience to Act):
To recruit a core constituency of 1000–1500 activists/volunteers for the work of Planet 3000 in six individual communities in order to promote the placement of a pilot program to test a key principle within the next two years.

Target Audience in Each of the Six Targeted Cities:
• Community leaders
• Youth
• Business leaders
• Local government officials
• Local union leaders
• Teachers

- Local reporters, editors, and producers
- Local environmental activists/organizations

Message(s):

In a world spinning out of control, a more balanced life is possible. Natural ecosystems have nurtured life on the planet for millions of years. Join Planet 3000 at Town Hall on October 1 to learn how the laws of nature can enhance your life and your community.

Strategies:

1. Have one-on-one meetings with key local activists/organizations to learn about community culture, concerns, and so on; follow up with breakfast briefings on the research project and interim findings.

2. Conduct mall intercepts in each city to test messages and measure depth of concern for issue(s); give out postcard handout with "more information" contact sites—for example, Web address, phone number, local groups—and key message take-away.

3. Schedule editorial board meetings with local newspaper and broadcast news groups.

4. Review local media to draft a framing memo on population and environmental issues as well as how scientific research is covered in the community.

5. Conduct a paid radio ad and billboard campaign.

6. Meet with local grocery store chains about imprinting shopping bags with our message.

7. Distribute instructional kits to biology and environmental study teachers of junior and senior high schools to use to develop in-class experiments; include feedback form for teachers to return to receive quarterly print updates on the project—"Update Planet 3000: Coming to Your Town." (Match information on Web site with links to local environmental information.)

8. Plan town hall meetings in six communities where experts can talk to interested citizens about natural law and human life in a nonthreatening setting. Broadcast the meetings either on cable access or the public television station. Videotape the meetings and make the videotapes available to schools as a launchpad for classroom discussion.

9. Follow up town hall meetings with a series of consensus-building meetings facilitated by a community leader trained in the nuances of

consensus building and the eco-human systems principles. (Have weeklong training for key facilitators from the six cities.)

Vehicles to Be Produced:

1. Briefing materials already prepared—fact sheet, nonacademic summaries of pilot project proposals, visual maps, purpose statement, and work plan for research project—but, inasmuch as possible, targeted to concerns/realities of the six local communities

2. Postcards

3. Framing memo

4. Radio ads

5. Billboard ads

6. High school instructional kits

7. Cover letter to biology/environmental studies teachers

8. Update Planet 3000: Coming to Your Town

9. Town hall meeting

10. Videotape

11. Facilitator training sessions

12. Consensus building follow-up sessions

EFFECTIVE COMMUNICATIONS HAPPEN OVER MEDIA, OVER TIME

Four things to remember as you build your plan and begin to take steps to implement various parts of it:

- Stay on message no matter which vehicle or strategy you choose
- Use vehicles that reinforce each other and build momentum
- Track what tasks need to be done, by when, and by whom
- Take advantage of current events but always have your plan

Calendar Tips
Be realistic. Work backward to ensure that your projects are doable given existing time and budget constraints as well as existing staff and volunteer commitments. Assign tasks to those people who have the knowledge to see

them through and stick to deadlines. A missed deadline creates chaos down the line!

Finally, as stories emerge within your community or as new events or activities are scheduled by your project group or others, make sure you note them on your calendar. Plan a Monday morning or Friday afternoon meeting to review the week's efforts (see Chapter 6). What new situations have surfaced relating to your objective and how could your organization build momentum from them? By regularly scheduling an active review of your communications plan and the evolving external situation as well as current media coverage, you'll be better positioned to take advantage of external events and news coverage to build momentum for your own communications activities, all of which will help you reach your objectives.

Exercise #8: Create the work plan. Assign target dates and tasks. [CH0501.DOC] Plot it out on a calendar.

CH0501.DOC

PLANNING WORKSHEET
STRATEGY AND TASK BREAKDOWN

__Communications Objective:__ _____

__Target Audience(s):__

Strategy/task	Target date	Person Responsible	Cost	Total cost per strategy

(Continued)

COMMUNICATIONS CALENDAR WORKSHEET

Using your strategy worksheet, write month, date, activity, and person
responsible for each task involved in implementing each strategy. Note
events, holidays, launch dates, and so on.

Month	Date	Action/task/event/holiday	Person Responsible

Step #6:
How to Make It Happen?

Turning Obstacles into Opportunities

There are four things that an organization must put in place to make a plan happen:

1. Organizational buy-in
2. Expertise
3. Time
4. Money

If any of these four components is missing, the communications plan eventually will run into trouble. It doesn't take a lot of effort to ensure that a solid foundation is in place; it only takes some attention to detail and, as with any plan, some effort on the part of the individual(s) spearheading the communications effort within the organization.

BUY-IN: CREATING ORGANIZATIONAL OWNERSHIP

There has to be a compelling reason for an organization to commit its resources to a new—that is, untried and untested—strategy or program. In many cases, this is a first hurdle to be jumped before any communications effort can move forward. Yet, the only way for a communications plan to be successful is if it has 100 percent buy-in from the entire organization—staff, board, and volunteers, especially if the organization's programs rely heavily on volunteers.

While it isn't necessary for everyone to understand all the details and the reasons why one strategy was chosen over another, people do need to see the connection between the communications plan and the organization's mission, goals, and objectives. Everyone will need to know the organization's messages so that he or she can communicate those messages in both professional and personal situations. Having everyone connected to the organization on message reinforces the message throughout and beyond the community in less "structured" or "official" ways, creating a ripple effect that extends beyond the people connected with the organization to everyone with whom they come in contact.

There are many ways to create buy-in for your organization's communications efforts. The first is to think of these internal constituencies as "audiences" in order to develop messages that will persuade them of the plan's importance (see Exhibit 6-1). While everyone will have the organization's best interests at heart, those interests may be defined very differently depending on a person's role in the organization. For example, the financial officer may be convinced by a message that stresses the plan as a way to leverage existing resources, while a program director may only be persuaded by a message that highlights the connection between communications and the organization's program objectives, regardless of the cost.

When "tweaking" your message to address the unique perspectives of the various individuals and groups from whom you'll need buy-in for the communications plan, always reinforce the idea that "communicating strategically will strengthen our organization and maximize our investment of time and money while having a positive impact on our program goals" (see Exhibit 6-2).

Exhibit 6-1.   Whose Buy-In Will You Need?

Executive director	Board of directors
Senior management	Line staff
Program staff	Administrative staff
Financial director	MIS staff
Volunteers	

Exhibit 6-2.   Persuasive Language for Internal Constituencies

What it is	Why it's important	What should I do?
Shared vision	Revenue	Get involved
Strategic	Strengthen organization	Learn about it
Tool	Job security	Support it
Plan for talking to people	Pride in organization	Help out
Measure of success	Edge over competition	Put it on the agenda
Social change	Improve public perception	Help reallocate resources
Window to what we do	More clients, donors, volunteers	Don't stand in the way
	Reposition the organization	
	Reframe the issue	
	Lend credibility to what we do	

The language you use to persuade internal constituencies of the importance of practicing strategic communications must resonate with them and their concerns.

In addition to presenting a forceful message, listening is a critical component of any buy-in strategy—not to debate a point that is made but rather to emphasize that everyone's ideas are valuable and that the process is an open one. Indeed, listening to what people say will equip you to better judge the degree of their commitment to the communications plan. In addition, hearing people's concerns may help you as you progress through the buy-in process because you will be able to anticipate and respond to those concerns—which, in the long run, will make the end result stronger and more representative of the entire organization.

Several strategies that might be used to create buy-in are suggested below. Obviously, any strategy should be tailored to your organizational culture as well as the communications preferences of the individual with whom you are communicating. Decide what strategy to use based on what has worked in the past when your organization has had to build teams, create consensus, develop strategic plans, or launch new program initiatives, and model your buy-in strategies around the methods that have a proven track record within your organization.

Possible Buy-In Strategies

1. Get it on the agenda at a senior management meeting. Work through a condensed version of the seven-step process. Encourage active participation and use the various questions throughout the book as a starting point for discussion. Especially focus on the situational analysis within which the organization functions, its objectives, audience characteristics, and message development—the foundation for any communications plan. Elicit management's thoughts on evaluation criteria—for example, what results would convince them that the communications effort was successful and worth the organization's investment of time and money.

2. Ask program staff members what their goals and objectives are for the year. Clarify these and make sure they are measurable, but don't mention communications at the outset. Then come back and explain how the communications objectives are an integral part of the program objectives and that specific groups of individuals are necessary in order for the staff to achieve success. Once staff members agree to that idea, explain that these groups are "audiences." Invite the staff to participate in a session on message development. Present a framing memo so that staff members can understand how an issue is currently being positioned in relation to what they are trying to accomplish.

3. Hold a meeting with line staff members to present the organization's objectives, audiences, and draft messages. Ask for their impressions and their feedback. By engaging the entire staff of the organization, you can not only create ownership of the process but also help ensure that all staff members are on board during implementation and roll-out, and that each understands that he or she is a "communicator" for the organization and its issues and realizes that by "singing from the same hymnbook" everyone reinforces the organization's vision and long-term goals.

4. Conduct a brief presentation for your organization's board of directors, summarizing the process and the results of the senior staff meeting. If you or a senior staff member doesn't feel completely comfortable answering technical questions, invite a consultant or volunteer who has experience in communications to attend the meeting. Make the case for a communications program by discussing what objectives would be addressed and what resources would be needed. Encourage questions, comments, and ideas. It is key that the board of directors understand and commit to this effort early on so that there

is a strong foundation of support through which staff members can feel confident as they begin to implement the plan.

5. Actively recruit volunteers who understand the importance of or have experience with communications to join a committee that can monitor issues in the media, help create messages, suggest evaluation criteria, and assess results. This type of volunteer effort will help validate your communications efforts within the larger organizational structure and also contribute time and energy needed to get the work done.

6. Have a regular column in the organization's newsletter to update staff and volunteers about the communications effort and its impact. Feature names of staff and/or volunteers who have helped make the effort a success as a way to recognize their work and to reinforce that the organization's communications effort belongs to everyone.

7. Communicate to the entire organization—staff and volunteers—on a regular basis about how various communications strategies have helped advance the organization's objectives. (This can be done via print—memos, newsletters—e-mail, voice mail updates, or face-to-face meetings.) Also keep staff, board, and volunteers informed on a regular basis (monthly) of what the current messages are. Provide these people with "talking points" so that they know how to frame issues in a way that maximizes the facts through analogy or comparison, uses emotional language, and recognizes the power of storytelling—in other words, that reflects the human, real-life implications of any issue.

Once a communications effort becomes part of the organization's culture and infrastructure, it becomes indispensable. Once it becomes indispensable, it becomes a part of everyone's day-to-day life; it is "what we do." Having people who are aware of the organization's communications efforts and who are committed to getting the message out in both their professional and personal lives means that the message—and the mission—will take root within the community and become a "matter of fact." In addition, by fostering this approach among everyone connected with the organization, the message and the commitment of these individuals to proactively communicate in a positive way about the organization on a regular basis will reinforce their dedication to the mission and to the issues with which the organization is involved.

Finally, this approach will ultimately ensure that the communications plan *will* happen because so many people will be intent on seeing it happen.

EXPERTISE: THE COMMUNICATIONS ACTION TEAM

All too often the individuals within the organization who are most enthusi-astic about pursuing a proactive communications plan don't reach out for help, or if they do, they ask those individuals who have the most on their plates and are hard-pressed to take on yet another commitment. Because a communications plan is a "living" thing—it isn't something that can be done this week and put away until next month—it will require ongoing effort on the part of those most directly involved in it. Even if it is only a single phone call or listserv posting, something will happen on a daily basis.

However, when more than one person actively participates not only in shaping the plan but also in performing the many tasks involved in making it happen, it is more likely that the organization will succeed. One way to secure the necessary proactive involvement is to create a communications action team (CAT) to be responsible for all facets of an organization's communications effort.

What the CAT Does

The CAT is in charge of doing the research on which to create the plan, or working with outside experts to have it done. It is responsible for building the plan and securing buy-in from other constituencies within the organiza-tion. The CAT also implements the plan—or supervises others who may be responsible for performing individual tasks that comprise the various strate-gies—and evaluates the effectiveness of the communications effort on a regu-lar basis in order to fine-tune and update the plan as needed (see Chapter 7).

The CAT will have to meet regularly—preferably once a week, because the communications environment is so fluid and fast-paced, but no less than once a month. This can be done via a conference call or in person. At these meetings, team members should review and reevaluate the different parts of the plan not only to update each other on how the plan is unfolding but also to change direction when necessary.

Who to Recruit

There are four things to consider when recruiting CAT members:

- Expertise or skills
- Attitude toward the organization's communications effort

- Character or personality traits
- Current responsibilities within the organization

See Exhibit 6-3 for an elaboration of the desired qualities of CAT members.

Different organizations—as well as the individuals "leading the charge" and advocating for the creation of a communications plan—will have different wish lists when it comes to who they would want on the CAT. That is why it is useful to brainstorm with others inside the organization as to who might best "fit in" with the team and be willing and able to do the work. Make a list of the variables in each category so that you can easily see what's important in creating a successful CAT. While you will want someone with a certain type of expertise or skills on the team, it may be that other qualities are just as important to the team's success. For example, an excellent writer who doesn't easily share his or her ideas with others may not be a good CAT member. In addition, you will want to recruit individuals from different departments or areas of the organization to ensure that all program goals—including internal communications—are being addressed within the communications plan.

Once you've noted the characteristics you want, consider the individuals within the organization—or others who might be interested in volunteering their time to the effort. Who embodies which traits, skills, and expertise? Once you've prioritized possible individuals for the CAT, invite them to join. If necessary, ask the person's supervisor beforehand whether it is possible to include this person in the CAT.

Exhibit 6-3.   Desired Qualities for CAT Members

Expertise/skills	Attitude	Character	Department/program
Interpersonal skills	Enthusiastic	Team player	Communications
Writing	Good listener	Committed to project	Development
Public relations	Meets deadlines	Creative	Government affairs
Technology	Passionate	Leadership	Administrative/MIS
Graphic design	Positive, "can-do"	Honest	Education
Has connections	Aware of the power of language, images, symbols	Self-motivated	Client services

The CAT core team should have at least three people, but the more people a team has, the more you can do. On the other hand, there will also be more of a need for coordination of logistics and calendar tracking with more people. If your CAT is large—more than seven people—you might want to consider breaking up the team into working groups that mix and match people according to strategies or objectives.

Once you've selected an individual based on the criteria you've identified as important for team members, use the following questions to guide your selection process.

Guiding Questions

- Can this person commit sufficient time and attention for at least six months?
- Is he or she comfortable as a team player?
- Can he or she take charge of a task and get it done without supervision?
- Does he or she usually meet deadlines?
- Is he or she interested in learning more about communications tools, techniques, and strategies?

 Exercise #9: List the characteristics, attitudes, and expertise you would like to have on your organization's CAT. Next, make a list of individuals—staff, board members, or volunteers—who embody a combination of several of these variables. Finally, prioritize these individuals based on the guiding questions. Invite them to join—or assign them to—the CAT. Remember to personalize the recruiting message to show how their work on the CAT will not only benefit the organization but also their own professional or personal growth.

TAKE THE TIME, MAKE THE TIME

Once the human resources are committed, setting aside the time to get things done is the next hurdle in making a communications plan a reality. The importance of making the time to plan, implement, and evaluate the communications effort cannot be stressed enough. Because a communications plan is a living thing—an ongoing process—one task that is delayed or postponed can derail an entire strategy. Thus, finding the time on an individual level becomes more important than allocating sufficient time within the plan itself. This is why commitment to the plan among all CAT members is imperative.

The most important rule in finding and making time is to have a written plan on a calendar, with a target date and a person assigned for each task. This puts that person on notice that "this Thursday, I have to get the alert out," enabling that person to plan his or her day accordingly.

On the other hand, there will always be a certain amount of fluidity, because even the best-laid plans can disintegrate into rushing to respond to an opportunity or challenge from the external environment that wasn't in the plan. For example, the Supreme Court hands down a decision for which your organization has been prepared. The contact database is ready to generate e-mail and broadcast fax messages. Someone has been at the Court waiting each morning for the last two weeks to get a copy of the Court's opinion. Legal counsel is back at the office, ready to analyze what it means to the organization, its constituents, and the country as a whole. A fax machine at an office near the court has been secured in order to fax the opinion to counsel. A press conference will be called, an impact statement with talking points will be broadcast to affiliates and coalition members, and interviews for the organization's spokesperson will be scheduled with reporters. All of this goes like clockwork, but phone calls from individuals asking, "What does this mean to me?" flood the organization much more rapidly than anyone had anticipated and no one is prepared to handle the onslaught.

No matter how prepared the CAT is, there usually will be one or more things that are unanticipated or left undone. However, even in this circumstance, a good communications plan ensures that as many pieces as can be put together beforehand are in place, helping what might otherwise be chaos seem only "terribly busy."

Another example of an unanticipated communications event might be played out if something tragic happened to a client. The press descends on the agency, perhaps even before the agency itself knows the details of what has happened to the individual. Again, while the crisis could not be foreseen, it could have been planned for in the generic sense—for example, "What will happen if a child whose case we are handling dies due to child abuse we didn't see?" Key messages woven into the very fabric of the organization and reinforced on a regular basis throughout the community will help lay the groundwork within the community as to how it perceives the organization and, through that perception, how it will respond to this type of crisis and the organization's recommendation to prevent future tragedies.

Tips for Finding Time

1. Turn your calendar into a checklist. Have CAT members mark the dates on their personal calendars for tracking.

2. Consider the seamlessness of every strategy. Sometimes it is more time efficient to put one person in charge of all the tasks involved with an entire strategy; at other times it is better to divide the tasks that make up a single strategy among several people who work well together.

3. Do one thing a day and do it first thing in the morning. Make your communications task a top priority so that, no matter what else happens during the day, the organization's communications effort remains on track.

MONEY: IF IT'S A GOOD IDEA, YOU CAN SELL IT

If reallocating existing money isn't enough to cover the cost of your plan and the CAT strongly agrees that the strategies it has chosen are the most cost effective it can use and still achieve the desired results, it will have to figure out how to raise the money from sources outside the organization. (Obviously, if an organization has a fund-raising staff or a board development committee, individuals from those groups would probably take the lead in raising these funds. Someone on the CAT should be involved in the fundraising effort.)

There are several sources to tap if your organization needs to raise additional money to make its communications plan a reality.

As with everything else, the key to raising the necessary financial support for your communications effort is to develop messages that will move the audience—in this case, grant makers, agency officials, or individual donors—to act. Show how these communications efforts connect to your program objectives and build your communications expenses into any program proposal used to raise money for a given program. Piggyback your argument on the fact that most grant makers—like government agencies—want an organization to disseminate information about the program or its results. Many acknowledge the importance of outreach to target populations. They want organizations to influence public policy as well as human behavior, attitudes, and opinions. In order to achieve these and many other goals, an organization must practice strategic communications, and it takes money to do that work—work that should be described as an integral part of the entire program in the proposal for which your organization is asking for funding.

Plain and simple: Your communications strategy is an integral part of your program. It has a direct effect on your organization's program success, and the cost of implementing those strategies must be seamlessly woven into grant proposals.

At the same time, learn to make your case to grant makers, business leaders, and individual donors. Now that you and your team understand the critical connection between your organization's goals, its audiences, and appropriate communications strategies, learn how to explain communications to these funders in a way that focuses on program and not on "making a video" or "publishing a newsletter." Don't be afraid to say: "These communications activities are crucial to our program's success and we need to be able to do this to accomplish our program goals."

Other Opportunities

Once you are in the midst of implementing your organization's communications plan, take advantage of opportunities that arise as a way to raise additional support for your efforts. For example, if your organization or its issues are featured in the mass media, consider piggybacking a targeted direct mail campaign to those audiences most likely to have been exposed to that media coverage. It doesn't have to be fancy—a letter from your president, your chairperson, or a spokesperson affiliated with your agency along with a clean copy of the clipping can be sent to high-dollar donors, business leaders, and others to solicit additional financial support for the effort.

Income-Producing Possibilities

Because part of the nonprofit mission is to educate targeted publics to create social change, nonprofits have tended to give away any and all information and knowledge that they produce. Yet, we are living in the Information Age. While information may be cheap, knowledge is valuable and products that result from that knowledge are also valuable. Your organization may want to explore how to charge certain publics for certain knowledge products that you're currently giving away and build that into your plan as well. Even something as simple as charging for the cost of printing and distribution to defray these out-of-pocket expenses can often mean the difference between being able to produce the product or not.

In-Kind Contributions

Finally, compile a list of nonfinancial contributions you could use to implement the strategies in your plan—equipment, professional services, printing, graphic design, postage, video editing and dubbing, and so on. Brainstorm with members of your staff or with a small pool of volunteers about businesses, corporations, large-membership organizations, and even public institutions that might be able to contribute this type of support. Then assign each person several contacts to talk to about nonfinancial support. Rehearse the group's message—why implementing this strategy is important to the success of your program and why that program is critical to the welfare of the community. It might also be useful to note whether there is a tangible or intangible benefit for the sponsors—that is, whether their assistance will be noted in information the program distributes. A word of caution when accepting in-kind contributions as a way to make any communications strategy affordable: always have the final approval of the work or service being contributed. For example, a brochure that is beautifully designed may be appealing to produce, but if it doesn't accurately reflect the organization as defined by its board of directors it will only cause more trouble than it's worth.

CONCLUSION: BET$

Putting these four elements into place before finalizing and launching any communications plan will prove to be critical to the plan's success and the degree of impact it will have on the organization, its programs, and the community it serves.

1. **Buy-in**
2. **Expertise**
3. **Time**
4. **$ (Money)**

If one of these four components are missing, all BET$ are off . . . or, at the very least, the odds will be against you.

CH0601.DOC

WORKSHEET FOR STEP #6

Organizational Buy-In

What does this communications effort mean to the organization? Write down as many reasons as you can think of; use single words or phrases to explore all possibilities.

_____	_____
_____	_____
_____	_____
_____	_____
_____	_____
_____	_____

On the first line, note why the communications effort is important to the following individuals whose buy-in is necessary. What does this communications effort mean to them? Their work? On the second line, note what you want them to do.

Executive director _____

_____

Board of directors _____

_____

Senior management _____

_____

Line staff _____

_____

(Continued)

Program staff   _____

_____

Administrative staff   _____

_____

Financial director   _____

_____

MIS staff   _____

_____

Volunteers   _____

_____

List ideas for buy-in strategies and note which audience might be best approached using each strategy.

Possible strategy	Who would respond to this strategy
_____	_____
	_____
	_____
_____	_____
	_____
	_____
_____	_____
	_____
	_____
_____	_____
	_____

Target date for buy-in work completed _____

Desired Qualities for CAT Members

Expertise/skills	Attitude	Character	Department/ program

Names of individuals for action team   What they bring to the team

_____

_____

_____

_____

_____

• Can he or she commit sufficient time and attention for at least six months?
• Is he or she comfortable as a team player?
• Can he or she take charge of a task and get it done without supervision?
• Does he or she usually meet deadlines?
• Is he or she interested in learning more about communication tools, techniques, and strategies?

CHAPTER SEVEN

Step #7: Is It Working?

Evaluate What Happens

The "final"—and perhaps the most difficult—step in what is truly an ongoing process is to evaluate your efforts. To do this, of course, you must have clearly defined your objectives. From this information, you can begin to shape the criteria you will use to evaluate your communications efforts. Questions you should ask yourself should center around the following key areas.

1. The targeted public(s)
   - How did you define your audience(s) with respect to their relationship to the organization and/or the issue?
   - What other characteristics were used to define this group?

2. Nature of the intended change
   - Can it be defined in a way that it is recognizable—for example, when the change happens, will you be able to confirm it by seeing a certain result?
   - Where on the scale of 1 to 10—with 10 being the intended change or result—was the targeted audience(s) at the outset? Where are they now? How do you know?

3. Specific knowledge, attitude, or behavior to be achieved

- What knowledge, attitude, or behavior did the audience(s) have or practice at the outset?

4. Amount of change desired
   - How did you define the degree of change desired in relation to the starting point of the audience(s)?

5. Target date

Learning whether something worked and, if possible, why it worked is critical to success in the long run—that is, successes can be replicated and repeated. Understanding why a strategy didn't achieve the anticipated results is just as important in order to fine-tune future strategies or, if necessary, revise your plan.

Twelve levels of implementation and impact criteria can help your organization identify which evaluation methods to use at different stages of the communications process. The first four are fairly easy to accomplish, since they involve counting tangible things. Measuring impact—criteria 5 through 12—is more difficult and requires expertise in research methodology and survey design. It is not unusual for an organization to bring in a consultant to help in structuring the evaluation process and/or to actually do the evaluation at regular intervals in the process. If your organization can afford to take this approach, make sure that the consultant teaches members of the CAT not just how to do the evaluation but why it is being done this way so that, in the future, members of the CAT become more familiar with the evaluation process. Even if CAT members never become expert evaluators themselves, this awareness will help them identify criteria during the planning process and build in methods for gathering and analyzing the information that corresponds to those criteria.

EVALUATION CRITERIA[1]

1. Number of messages sent and activities planned—distribution, effort expended, resources committed

2. Number of messages placed in media and activities enacted—coverage, media mix, content, duration, gross impressions, potential exposures

---

[1] Modified from G. M. Broom and D. M. Dozier, *Using Research in Public Relations: Applications to Program Management*. Englewood Cliffs, NJ: Prentice-Hall, 1990.

3. Number who receive messages/participate in activities—reach, circulation, potential audience size

4. Number who attend to messages/activities—readership, viewership, listenership, attendance, frequency

Impact Begins Here

5. Number who learn message content—increased knowledge, awareness, and/or understanding

6. Number who change opinions

7. Number who change attitudes

8. Number who behave in desired fashion

9. Number who repeat behavior

10. Program objective achieved

11. Program goal achieved

12. Social and cultural change

Methods to evaluate the preparation stages of the organization's communications planning process should be added to these twelve levels of implementation and impact evaluation.

- Quality of message presentations—style, format, packaging
- Appropriateness of message content and organization of information
- Adequacy of background information—intelligence research—on which decisions were made

With this said, it should be noted that the true impact of an organization's communications activities is very hard to measure because, even with the best evaluation tools and the most stringent methodology, it is difficult to isolate one organization's communications program effects from other factors that may affect the awareness, knowledge, attitudes, and behavior of targeted audiences.

EVALUATION TOOLS

The next step is to figure out what methods to use to gather the information or data that will allow you to measure the effect of your communications efforts. Three standard approaches are discussed.

Focus Groups: Evaluating the Preparation Stage

The adequacy of background information has been covered in earlier chapters on situational analysis and targeting your audience (see Chapters 1 and 2). Testing messages at the concept stage as well as evaluating different ways to organize and present information is usually done through the use of focus groups.

In a focus group, the moderator (and observers who usually are not in the room and thus do not unduly influence the responses of the participants) attempts to make sense out of "thousands upon thousands of relevant observations—observations of nuance and feeling, of depth of feeling and conviction, of facial expression and body movement, of conflict, ambivalence, and paradox, and of attitudes, beliefs and needs."[2] Obviously, this isn't an easy task. It requires someone with good listening skills who is also adept at reading body language, at letting people talk without trying to control the discussion, and at judging and responding to the mood shifts of a group as well as of individuals as they are happening.

Focus groups can be a useful tool when an organization wants to know how members of a key audience perceive the organization and its work. They can also be used to get feedback on plans for future programs or activities. Issues of importance to the organization can be discussed by participants so that the organization can better understand the target audience's attitudes and values, which will color its reception of any message the organization delivers. Finally, focus groups can be used as a way to identify emerging problems or opportunities.

Participants are selected from the target audience population and pre-screened, usually over the phone, using questions to ensure that the person qualifies as a member of the target audience. A focus group usually has seven to twelve participants and a moderator who leads the group in a discussion using active listening techniques. Frequently a stimulus such as a drawing, slide, storyboard, or video clip is used to initiate the discussion. By asking for—and listening carefully to—the reactions of participants to the stimulus, the moderator begins building a rapport with the group. This first stage of the process is followed by an *exploratory* phase, at which time the moderator will pose very general, open-ended questions. In this way, the group helps define the dialogue that will occur during the remainder of the focus group. Next comes the *probing* phase. This is when the moderator hones in on more specific ideas, words, phrases, images, and so on in order to elicit a response from the participants. This information can be used to craft messages that employ language or images that reflect the target audience's sensibility. Participants are then asked to write or create something—

[2] H. Mariampolski, "The resurgence of qualitative research," *The Public Relations Journal*, 40(7), 1984, p. 21.

such as a slogan, a picture, or a replica of something using common house-hold objects—during the *task* phase. The purpose of this phase is to better understand what resonates with people like the participants—for example, the target audience. This is followed by an *evaluation* stage, at which time the participants are asked to evaluate a specific message, treatment, media product, or representation of an idea. The wrap-up—or *closing*—stage gives participants a chance to add anything else to the discussion that might not have come out earlier.[3]

Some researchers have objected to the focus group methodology, saying that it is too directive and doesn't allow participants the chance to talk about the topic in their own language and on their own terms. One response to this criticism is the intensive cultural interview. Like traditional focus groups, this method brings together a group of participants from the target audience(s). Instead of a guided discussion, however, these participants are asked to complete a task without the interference of a moderator. Observers then look for "mind-sets"—clusters of beliefs, attitudes, and knowledge—within the group that can be culturally defined. These mind-sets are then used to shape the messages and strategies that will be targeted to the audience represented by the group.[4]

Once messages have been tested and reformulated, groups with additional resources may want to survey a larger sample of the target audience(s) to measure the reaction to various messages, because the results from focus groups cannot—and should not—be extrapolated conclusively to the larger population.

Clipping Services and Analysis: Evaluating the Implementation Stage

> When a program does not work, an examination of placements may help detect what went wrong. When a program does work, as indicated by the impact evaluation, the analysis of placements is an integral aspect of understanding why it worked.[5]

The first part of this evaluation process is collecting the clips—preferably both print and electronic. One way to do this is for the organization to con-

---

[3] The six phases of a focus group as outlined by Mariampolski and cited in Dozier and Repper, *Excellence in Public Relations and Communications Management,* edited by James E. Grunig. Hillsdale, NJ: Lawrence Erlbaum Associates, 1992, p. 192.
[4] More information on this technique can be obtained from Planmetrics Cultural Analysis Group, 110 East 59 Street, New York, NY 10022.
[5] "Research Firms and Public Relations Practices," Dozier and Repper, p. 194.

tract with a clipping service for print media as well as a service to track broadcast media. Another way is to assign various media to staff and volunteers who commit to scanning one or several publications and/or radio, television, or cable stations on a daily basis in order to collect any coverage that occurs on the organization and the issues with which it is involved. (Remember: Don't overlook trade or specialized media as well as the more general media when doing this type of scan.)

There are several ways to analyze clips in an effort to evaluate the implementation phase of your communications plan:

- Volume of coverage—how much was written or how many minutes were aired

- Messages sent versus messages placed—number of press releases, phone calls, interviews, and so on that resulted in actual coverage

- How often the coverage accurately reflected your message or message frame

The next part of the process is to categorize coverage by media outlet—specific publication or radio or television program—as a way to evaluate which audiences you've reached and how many times they were exposed to the message. This is done by merging the data from your clipping analysis with data from secondary sources—audience characteristics and circulation/TV-radio ratings or audience share—which can be obtained directly from the media outlet. (Electronic publications, such as Web sites, will be able to tell you the number of "hits" a page has had but usually won't be able to give you much information as to audience characteristics.)

By combining the data from these two sources, you can begin to evaluate how often your organization's message was delivered to which populations. Obviously, this does not necessarily mean that that audience actually received and understood the message—for example, audience members may subscribe to the daily newspaper but that doesn't guarantee that they've read the article that included your message or that they understood and retained the message. For this, you must go one step further and look at readership, listenership, and viewership *surveys.*

The final way in which clips can be used to evaluate your communications efforts is by analyzing the content of the coverage. To do this, study individual sentences, paragraphs, or stories.

- Is it positive, negative or neutral?
- Are specific themes (frames) featured or not?
- What adjectives are used? What does this tell us about the coverage?

- Was the coverage news, editorial, letters to the editor, feature story, or some other type?

By doing this type of content analysis, you can judge how the target audience exposed to this coverage perceives the importance of issues and/or the organization in relation to those issues and the community in which it operates. (This is because mass media coverage translates into importance in the publics who read, view, or listen to those media.) Over time, this information can be used to spot trends—both evolutionary and static—that may be useful in modifying your messages or strategies for the future.

Finally, it should be noted that this type of evaluation, while extremely useful, should not be confused with impact. In many circumstances—especially when dealing with issues that generate extreme emotions among targeted audiences—positive or negative content may not necessarily translate in the audience's mind to a positive or negative message. If someone feels extremely negative about an issue, positive treatment in the media probably cannot guarantee a change of heart!

Sampling Surveys: Evaluating Impact

A basic tool of impact evaluation is surveys using methods that help guarantee that the sample is representative of the audience group at large. (The findings can be extrapolated to the whole population with a certain amount of accuracy.) This type of survey activity does not necessarily have to be in the form of a questionnaire. A review of routine organizational records that track the activities of key publics—such as phone logs, case files, social indicators, even the wear and tear on carpets where targeted audiences travel—can be used to help evaluate the program's success at some level. The added advantage of this approach is that the audience isn't aware that there is an evaluation process taking place during the course of its interaction with the organization.

There are two caveats to using surveys effectively to evaluate the impact of a communications program: (1) if it is impossible to survey the entire audience group, probabilistic sampling techniques must be used, and (2) more than a single survey should be used to measure impact.[6]

The most important factor is to ensure that the audience sample is truly "probabilistic" and not just a random part of the audience that is convenient to survey—for example, people who choose to respond, which makes the sample a self-selected one. To ensure that the survey results can be extrapolated to the larger audience population, the sample must:

---

[6] Dozier and Repper, "Research Firms and Public Relations Practices," Dozier and Repper, p. 201.

- Be random
- Be systematic—every *n*th person
- Follow rules of margins of error/level of confidence
- Preferably comprise 1000 or more respondents

During the survey design phase, a professional researcher can be of tremendous help and, if at all possible, an organization should hire someone or recruit a volunteer who can help the staff through this process. In order to evaluate the effectiveness of a communications program, there has to be a before and after test—otherwise it will be impossible to measure what if any change has occurred in opinions, attitudes, values, or behavior. However, as previously mentioned, it is difficult to measure the impact of the organization's activities in a vacuum; the external environment also has an effect on the audience one way or another. Because of this, the evaluator will try to identify a control group against which to compare the audience sample that has been exposed to the organization's efforts. Researchers can help an organization design tools that minimize or eliminate the influence of external factors (inasmuch as possible) in order to more accurately measure the effect of the organization's communications efforts.[7]

Traditional research, which is often associated with the practice of communications, may not always provide the type or quality of information we need to evaluate our efforts. For example:

Opinion polling often offers untrustworthy projections for a number of reasons—everything from respondents giving what they think is the "culturally correct" answer to the fact that someone can have an opinion about one issue that clashes with an opinion about another issue, making it difficult to anticipate the underlying values and beliefs as well as how the individual will act in a given situation.

Academic research often seeks underlying theoretical causes, rather than data that has immediate application to the practice of communications. So, while academic research on a specific issue or social problem may be used to inform an organization's communications efforts, it might not be useful in evaluating the impact of the communications program on a regular basis while the plan is unfolding.

Market research seeks common denominators or norms among large, diverse publics who are potential purchasers of a product or subscribers to an idea or position. Marketers don't care specifically who they convince as long as the projected market share is achieved.

---

[7] For more information on designing communications impact evaluation tools, see Broom and Dozier.

OTHER EVALUATION METHODS TO CONSIDER[8]

Open-ended questions that provide verbatim responses. Researchers dislike these because they're harder to code and analyze compared to predetermined response options. But nothing rivals respondents' own words.

Survey feedback. This is a basic data-gathering method in which a facilitator interviews group members or key decision makers individually, then feeds back results anonymously to the group. This method provides rich data that objectivizes emotion, lets people know they are heard, shows where positions are shared or dissimilar, and stimulates collaborative decisions.

Rolling research. Rather than surveying the entire sample at one time, with this method interviews are spread out at key intervals (quarterly, monthly, and so on). This provides a measure of change over time and allows comparison that shows direction.

800 numbers. This works better than a random sample because it sorts out those who feel strongly enough to do something, that is, call. When responses are charted, comparison over time gives valuable data—as do topics discussed and semantics used by callers.

"Agree and disagree" asked. This response category captures a cell of opinion that is often determinative—since respondents who both agree and disagree on a point have clearly given thought to the subject. In addition to noting who agrees, disagrees, and doesn't know, this adds "both agree and disagree," and then records the reasons.

Some questions are suggested below to stimulate your thinking about how your organization might evaluate its communications program during the planning stages as well as periodically during implementation.

Guiding Questions

- What type of feedback do we need to assess the impact of our efforts? How will we obtain this feedback?

- What can we measure that would indicate that our activities are getting us closer to our objectives?

---

[8] Pat Jackson, "PR Needs Its Own Research Modes, Not Borrowed Ones," *PR Reporter,* 36(1), January 4, 1993; PR Publishing, P.O. Box 600, Exeter, NH 03833, (603) 778-0514. Used with permission.

- Are we meeting our target dates? If not, will we have to scale everything back?

- Are we ahead of our timetable? Is this an opportunity for us to speed up the process or does it indicate that things are spinning out of control?

- Are we reaching our target audience with this strategy? How can we tell?

- What methods can we set in place that will enable us to regularly measure the number of messages (1) sent and planned; (2) placed or enacted; (3) received; (4) attended to (evaluation criteria 1–4)?

- How can we measure the number or percentage of our target audience(s) who learn the content of the message? Can we clearly describe for ourselves what "learning the content of the message" means for us? If so, what methods might we use to find that out?

- Aside from questionnaires, what nontraditional ways might we use to measure changes in opinions, attitudes, behavior—for example, cleaner streets, worn carpets, community health indicators?

- How do we plan to evaluate whether the measurable objective was achieved? Can we use any of those measures in evaluating our communications efforts?

- How do we define "social and cultural change" in light of our communications work? Can we simplify it so that we know clearly and easily what it is we are working toward? Will we know it when we see it? If yes, what does that mean?

GETTING IT DONE

Finally, a problem most organizations have to face is the lack of resources—and lack of expertise within the organization—to handle the evaluation process. There are creative ways to leverage existing resources for evaluation, but you should also remember to factor this into your program budgets and fundraising proposals. Evaluation isn't an afterthought or an option; it is necessary in order to be effective as communicators.

Some ways to help defray the cost of evaluation are present in the information-gathering stages:

1. Use volunteers. Create an interview tool and let the volunteers phone from home. Put together a volunteer focus group representing differ-

ent audience groups to help you understand the position of your various audiences.

2. Recruit help from local corporations, public relations firms, or advertising agencies that have strategic planning/market research departments in house.

3. Find ways to piggyback your communications evaluation onto the work the organization is already doing to evaluate programs, which is already funded as part of the quality control of managing and developing successful programs. If your organization has an evaluation budget, make sure part of it gets tied to evaluating communications efforts.

4. Get together with other organizations that share similar issues or interests to share the cost. You may be better able to afford an outside consultant who can study attitudes, opinions, and behaviors of the same audience groups for different issues or several audience groups on a single issue of concern to all the partnering organizations.

PUTTING THE LESSONS TO WORK

While it is important to be able to prove to funders, the board of directors, and others with a stake in the organization's work that your communications efforts are succeeding, it is even more important to use the information you gather through the evaluation process to fine-tune and improve your plan. How this is done will vary according to the data you collect, what you are trying to achieve, and what the data tells you about what you are trying to achieve.

Always schedule sufficient time—at least a couple of hours—for a CAT meeting soon after any data analysis becomes available. At that time, look at the elements of your plan and judge whether, according to the latest information, it is still viable and relevant to your objectives and your goals. The questions below are not exhaustive; rather, they are meant to guide and stimulate you in putting what you learn in the evaluation process to work for you in your future and ongoing communications plan.

Audience: Has it expanded? Contracted? Redefined itself? Are there subsets that can be managed more efficiently than the whole? Are different audiences coming together to create one larger group with whom the organization could more cost-efficiently communicate?

Message: Is the message being delivered to the target audiences? If not, why not? If yes, what treatment did it receive? Is the message staying intact? Can members of the audience recall the message? Is the language used in the message resonating with the target audience? Is it being used by third parties to discuss the issue?

Strategy: Is the strategy reaching the target audience? Is it having the desired effect? Which strategies are working? Why? Are there other strategies that are similar in nature to be successful ones that could be repeated or replicated?

By understanding not only what's working and what's not but also how to use that information to modify, reposition, or revise our plan, we keep our communications plan alive—it truly becomes a process—which is what the practice of communications, when done well, is all about.

> A worksheet is provided on the disk to help you conduct the
> [CH0701.DOC] evaluation of the communications plan.

CONCLUSION

Evaluating your organization's communications efforts will not be easy, but it is necessary to being effective in the long run. It is a relatively new area being explored by many practitioners and academics alike, so don't get frustrated or set up unrealistic expectations. Be clear about what information you can and will gather—having doable measures is better than a plan to collect data that is impossible—or too expensive—to undertake. Make sure you budget for evaluation work, because even the most basic methods—for example, analysis of clips—will take time and money. Set target dates on your calendar for the evaluation process and the analysis report with the most appropriate member of the CAT having supervisory responsibility. Be creative in defining measures of success based on your measurable objectives and get help from those individuals who are evaluating other aspects of the organization's program. Although the evaluation measures or techniques may be different, the effects to be measured may shed some light on the impact of your communications work. Finally, use the evaluation data and analysis to inform the ongoing communications planning process. As people absorb a message and begin to modify their opinions or beliefs, new messages will have to be developed and new strategies put in place. You can only know when to do this if you've been evaluating what is happening in the external environment, especially as it concerns your target audiences.

CH0701.DOC

EVALUATION: MEASURING SUCCESS

Time Period Being Evaluated:_____

1. Total number of messages sent _____

2. Total number of activities planned _____

3. Messages sent by medium

    Total print:_____

    Total audio:_____

    Total video:_____

    Total electronic:_____

    Total face-to-face: _____

4. Total number of messages placed in media not controlled by organization/media mix

Type of coverage	Gross impressions/ potential exposures	Percentage of total coverage
_____	_____	_____
_____	_____	_____
_____	_____	_____
_____	_____	_____
_____	_____	_____
_____	_____	_____
_____	_____	_____
_____	_____	_____

Content Analysis

What were the major messages conveyed?

How was the issue framed and who had control of the framing?

What words appeared repeatedly?

Was our message part of the mix?

---

5. Number who received messages (based on circulation, reach of media):

_____

Number who attended to messages (readership, viewership, listenership):

_____

6. Number who participated in activities: _____

How often (attendance, frequency)? _____

Impact Evaluation: What Are Some Areas We Can Measure That Would Help Us Identify Changes That Have Occurred, in Part because of Our Efforts?

Number who learned message content – increased knowledge, awareness, understanding

- What do we mean by this?

- What can we look at to measure it?

- What method can we use to obtain this information?

Number who changed opinions

- What question(s) can we ask to measure the opinions of the audience(s) before and after?

- What methods can we afford to use to ask the question(s)?

- Are there other forms of information that would indicate this type of change?

Number who changed attitudes

- What question(s) can we ask to measure the attitudes of the audience(s) before and after?

- What methods can we afford to use to ask the question(s)?

- Are there other forms of information that would indicate this type of change?

Number who behaved in desired fashion

- How do we define this?

- Aside from asking the question – to which the audience member might or might not give an honest answer – what else could we measure that would tell us that someone is taking a certain action?

Number who repeated behavior
- How do we define this – over how long a period of time is the behavior repeated?

- Aside from asking the question – to which the audience member might or might not give an honest answer – what else could we measure that would tell us whether someone is repeating a certain behavior or performing a certain action on a regular basis?

Program objective achieved
- Area of change realized?

- Target audience reached?

- Nature/direction of the change accomplished?

- Degree of change accomplished?

- Time frame or target date met?

Program goal achieved
- Where is the target population with respect to the program goal now as opposed to when we set that goal?

- How will we know when our program goal is achieved?

- What can we measure that would reflect progress toward the goal?

Social and cultural change
- How are we defining this?

- What will it look like?

- What social indicators can we use to measure this change?

- What systems could we study that would reflect change in this area?

The Time Is Now

Whether you manage to work through all of the exercises or not, you are hopefully more informed about the communications process and will put into practice at least some of the ideas in this book. This method, taught at dozens of workshops, has a proven track record of success. To many it may appear straightforward and simple. It is. As human beings, we communicate every day without giving it a second thought. To others the method may appear complicated. It is. The environment in which we communicate is complex and chaotic, with millions of voices struggling to be heard.

There are a few guarantees, however, to leave you with. The more your organization puts into its communications effort, the more it will benefit from those efforts and the greater success it will realize. If you have a plan, chances are very good that it will actually happen. And, nothing is constant but change. Your plan is fluid and must be regularly reevaluated and adapted to what is happening *now*.

In the words of Charles Buxton, "You will never 'find' time for anything. If you want time, you must make it." There is no time like the present to begin.

Hiring Consultants and Technical Assistance Providers

If your organization decides to hire a consultant or technical assistance provider (TAP), contact several to discuss your communications need. If you have a fixed budget, let the providers know that. Some nonprofit managers are wary of letting providers know their budgets because they think the providers will bid up to those budgets even if the service costs less. However, if you let providers know you're seeking other bids, there is less chance of that occurring. And you may find either that you've underpriced the project or that you'd be wasting your time and the provider's if you pursued the conversation.

If the initial phone discussion confirms that the TAP can provide the services within your budget, ask for a meeting to discuss the specifics of your project. Use the meeting to get a better sense of what a working relationship would be like for your organization. Here's a checklist to help you do this.

1. Look at examples of past work for quality, style, and results.

2. Get a feel for the person(s) that would be involved in delivering the service and whether you think you can work with him or her. The person(s) you'll be working with directly may not always be the same person(s) making the presentation at the initial meeting.

3. Clarify the process for your mutual involvement in the project's development and decision making. This is a good time to discuss how much of your time or your staff's time will be needed for the project.

4. Lay out a timetable for the project. Obviously, this may change as the project gets defined more clearly (which may not happen at the initial meeting), but the provider should be able to map out how quickly things can be accomplished.

5. Determine how the provider normally formalizes its relationship with clients; for example, by signed contract.

6. Learn how the providers get compensated—for example, monthly payments or portions of the total on benchmark delivery dates—and how they handle out-of-pocket expenses and overhead charges.

7. Find out how the providers set a price for the service (flat rate versus hourly or daily charge). Also ask about the possibility of overruns, and what penalties—for example, discounts on the fee—you can expect if the project is delayed.

8. Discuss how you will measure the success of the project.

9. Make sure there are points at which you can cancel the contract if dissatisfied.

If you don't know what kind of help you need, this process may seem more open-ended and risky. Remember, when you go to a widget salesman, you are likely to see the world and your communications need—whatever it is— through the lens of widgets. Who do you go to if you don't know whether you need widgets or doodads? Maybe you think you want more media coverage of your organization, but what may make more sense is a targeted ad campaign or community outreach. You have several audiences you want to reach, but aren't sure what the best outlets are for reaching them: Special events? Public service advertising? Radio or TV or print? Video news releases or press conferences? You need to find a provider that can help you think through the options and then plan, and perhaps implement, an effective communications strategy. There are providers who know how to work under such conditions and can help clarify your goals. Look for providers who fall into the broadest expertise category—communications analysis—or who cover a range of expertise. (See the glossary in Appendix B for help in defining what each area of expertise means.)

Remember, however, that if the only deliverable is a plan for addressing a particular communications objective, you will need to figure out, preferably in advance, how you will judge its adequacy. Also be clear as to the extent of the service: Is the provider capable of helping you implement the plan once it's formulated or will the provider recommend someone else? Finally, when you meet with any provider, consider how the provider will match your organization's culture and attitude. For instance:

- Does the provider seem to understand your organization's needs, resources, and opportunities?

- Is the provider sensitive to your style of operating or your constituency's concerns?

- Does the provider seem to offer creative, new approaches to your communications problems?

- How well have other organizations worked with the provider under similar circumstances?

After you have met with a few providers about your current needs, you should contact at least two references to get a better idea of what to expect should you choose to work with that particular provider. This reference check will also inform further discussion with the TAP before you contract for specific services.

Whatever provider you end up selecting, you'll want to make sure that communication between your organization and the provider is regular and clear, and, when appropriate, in writing. You will want to make sure someone in your organization is assigned to supervise the provider and move the project along. This will ensure that each of you has realistic expectations and the ability to adjust to external or internal changes.

OTHER LOCAL RESOURCES

There are other local resources that can help your organization meet a variety of communications needs. These organizations may have meeting or video facilities that they make available to nonprofits free of charge. Or they may help you produce a public service announcement or a video, design and print a brochure, or help you formulate a communications plan. Many of these resources have either excess capacity to donate to nonprofit projects or executives who can volunteer their time. Although not every resource listed is available in every community, many nonprofits have accomplished a variety of communication projects by accessing one or more of the following types of resources.

Cable access centers

Community colleges

Corporate facilities

Mentors or loaned executives

Large national nonprofits

Local broadcast stations

Media arts centers

Public libraries

Glossary of
Communications Expertise

Advertising Develops messages and information that are controlled by the originating or sponsoring organization. These can be disseminated via either print or electronic media. Production and placement can be either paid for or donated (as with public service announcements).

Audio production Produces messages and information that are disseminated via audio materials such as radio spots, audio cassettes, and news actualities. Production usually includes coordinating and supervising all technical aspects of the development of the materials and may include scriptwriting and hiring of talent.

Communications analysis, planning, and consultation Uses an organization's program goals to assess communications needs. From that information, a strategy is developed with a plan for implementation.

Computer communications consulting and services Uses an organization's program goals as well as information needs and current resources to develop a plan for using computers for communicating through electronic mail, conferencing capabilities, the Internet, local area networks, and databases. Services may also include programming and/or training.

Conference planning   Handles logistics as well as program design and scheduling of a conference or a meeting.

Desktop publishing   Executes the layout of a publication through the use of computer software generically defined as desktop publishing software.

Direct mail   Develops and distributes materials through bulk mail to targeted mass audiences, usually using market research to determine audience groups.

Film production   Uses film to produce public service announcements, documentaries, and educational programs. Production usually includes coordinating and supervising all technical aspects of the development of the film and may include script writing and hiring of talent.

Graphics and design   Designs materials that may either comprise only text or incorporate images as well as words, such as page or video frame layout, logo development, and corporate identity campaigns.

Marketing analysis, planning, and consultation   Analyzes an organization's current position with respect to its program goals to determine which areas it should build, maintain, harvest, and terminate in light of the people who have an actual or potential interest in the organization's products, services, social policy developments, and so on.

Market research   Generates, transmits, and interprets feedback information originating in the environment relating to the success of the organization's marketing plans and strategies employed in implementing those plans.

Media advocacy   Uses the electronic and print media in a strategic way to advance social or public policy initiatives.

Media relations   Develops and fosters media contacts through telephone conversations, press releases and statements, interviews, press briefings and conferences, and dissemination of factual materials such as press kits, fact sheets, and so on.

Publications development   Uses an assessment of program goals and of the audience groups the organization wants to reach to develop print materials such as flyers, newsletters, reports, brochures, and so on. May also include actual design and creation of product.

Public relations   Develops and fosters an organization's image and reputation through direct contact with the public. This ranges from answering letters to giving speeches to conducting special events.

Special events   Coordinates events that are held for the public, such as rallies, auctions, receptions, and conferences, with the intention of advancing an organization's program goals.

Spokesperson training   Trains an organization's leader to succinctly define his or her message and persuade others about the organization's mission or position; usually includes rehearsing how one communicates in a variety of settings such as public speeches, meetings with community leaders, interviews with journalists, and testimony before legislative committees.

Telemarketing   Solicits contributions and/or sales over the telephone.

Telephone communications consulting and services   Uses an organization's program goals as well as information needs and current resources to develop a plan for using specialized telephone services, such as 800 or 900 numbers, fax, audiotext, and audioconferencing.

Videoconferencing   Conducts a multisite meeting by connecting participants through video and audio.

Video production   Uses video to produce materials such as public service announcements for television, documentaries, educational programs, and video news releases. Production usually includes coordinating and supervising all technical aspects of the development of the video program and may include script writing and hiring talent.

Cut Through the Clutter with Tiered Information

We've all heard the ad message: "I want my MTV." Implicit in this message (and its delivery) is: "And I want it NOW."

People today feel overwhelmed with information, which only increases the frustration they feel when it comes to finding the information they're looking for. Even when someone is doing a search on a database, it can be difficult to latch onto that one gem of information they need. Everywhere we look, the volume of information stands ready to overwhelm us.

- Stacks of files, mail, paper, phone messages, e-mail, and faxes clutter our offices.

- Our mailboxes overflow with direct mail solicitations, bills, magazines, and catalogs, although we rarely receive a letter or postcard from a friend.

- We read the daily newspaper, watch the evening news, listen to drive-time talk shows, pick up our favorite book.

- And don't forget all those things we should read, we should see, we should take the time to think about. . . .

This is the dilemma of the Information Age. It is something each of us lives with and the climate that most of the people we want to reach live within.

Because of this, there is a tremendous need for us to become editors of the information, to search out expert packagers and producers for our messages. We need to think of new ways to "cut" the information we want our audiences to see, hear, read, and think about. As people try to cut through the clutter, "tiered information" with easy-to-use indexing schemes or searching capability will become more desirable.

For example, one tiered approach that uses fax broadcast and fax on demand would be to fax broadcast a single list of articles available that week or highlights from five or six stories. Anyone interested in more information can call a number and retrieve the document, which is automatically sent from a fax-on-demand system. This allows individual readers to get specific, up-to-date information when they want it. In addition, this approach allows the information provider the chance to update a single document without having to revise an entire book or report. Plus, valuable data on the specific information that callers to the fax-on-demand system are interested in can be collected and analyzed. This helps the information provider plan for future.

What are some ways to implement a tiered information approach?

1. Once you have an information base, it is to your organization's advantage to use all the communications options available. By mixing and matching different vehicles, you're more likely to be able to provide your information and deliver your message in the way an audience member most wishes to receive it. For example, you can design a vehicle—such as a fax—with the bare essentials on one page while developing a longer piece as a newsletter article, a document in a fax-on-demand system, or an entry in a searchable database. Different vehicles can provide different amounts of information. This is one way you can be more responsive to your audience's information needs and very real time constraints. Nowadays, *less* information is *more* likely to be read, and getting a "foot in the door" is the first step to further engagement.

2. Always design for the vehicle you're using. Take the time to "program" your medium—whether it is a fax, a written report, a video, or a Web page. Give some thought to what looks good; what's the most important single piece of information; and how you can set it apart from the rest, so that it brings the reader or viewer further into the piece. A common mistake is producing something in one medium and then just "copying" it into another.

3. Over time, figure out which individuals prefer which types of vehicles. How much information do they want from you? How much do

they need? Give them the opportunity to access what they want when they want it. Begin with your board members, then go on to volunteers, clients, and supporters. Next, consider your outreach partners and individual reporters. These are audiences with whom you have an existing relationship and, because of this, your organization can benefit tremendously by being more responsive to the way they receive and process information. Keep this information in a database so that you can access it as you develop different types of vehicles. Your audience will appreciate and respond to your efforts.

A simple real-life case study illustrates this point. A person received a phone solicitation for a donation. The individual told the telemarketing representative that he preferred to receive information in the mail. A week later a letter from the executive director arrived, apologizing for the incident and indicating it wouldn't happen again. Understandably, the supporter was amazed not only to get the letter but also at the fact that there was no request for a donation. It was a simple acknowledgment that the individual's wishes had been noted. His response: "This group knows what it's doing. I'll definitely make a donation." The actual direct mail appeal followed a week later and a contribution was made.

This is a great example of strategic communications: the combined power of technology, tiered information—two messages delivered separately instead of in one piece—and an organization's responsiveness to an audience member.

Vehicle Options

PRINT

The first purpose of any written communication is to be read.

Digby Whitman

✔ Print, by its very nature, is a one-way medium and, for the most part, a solitary experience for individual audience members that can have an effect on the level of intimacy with the producer as it is perceived by the recipient.

✔ Print engages two senses: vision and touch.

✔ Print materials do not allow real-time interaction with audience members; there are no physical cues.

✔ In our society, print has achieved an extremely high comfort level for both producer and reader/viewer.

✔ Except for transit ads or billboards, print pieces are usually portable; audience members can take such pieces with them and consider the information "at their convenience."

✔ When used alone, print vehicles rely on visual impact and delivery method to command attention. Once the attention is caught, other elements sustain it. Over time, certain print materials will grab and hold attention simply because a relationship has been established between the audience and the producer of the print materials—for example, an organization, *The New York Times*, *Utne Reader*.

✔ Because a person can read a print piece at his or her own pace, print has a unique capacity for handling and presenting details, complex facts, statistical data, and in-depth information, making it manageable for the reader to absorb, analyze, and understand. It is arguably the best way to present budgets or financial statements, statistical data or academic theories, scientific research, or legal arguments.

✔ Nonprofits rely on print vehicles more frequently than other types of media to create and nurture relationships with various audience groups—donors, activists, members, and so on.

Positive Attributes

- Easily accessible to most audiences
- Familiar and easy to use
- Able to express details more fully than other media
- Usually portable
- Real time doesn't matter
- Ability to use words and graphics

Negative Attributes

- Limited use with illiterate population
- No physical cues
- No audio
- No interaction
- Ability to broadcast message, but usually at a high cost—often distribution must be added to production cost

Types of Print Vehicles Available

Press releases	Editorials, op-eds
Newspapers	Rolodex cards
Trade magazines	Letters to the editor

General interest magazines	Articles (reprints)
Brochures	Flyers, handbills
Cartoons	Feature stories
Billboards	Posters
Books	Curricula
Newsletters	Case studies
Reports	Surveys
White papers	Fact sheets
Stationery	Business cards
Calendars	Comic books

Advertising—transit, PSAs, newspapers, magazines

Print (with Delivery via Phone Lines): Faxes

Unique Attributes in Addition to Those Previously Mentioned for Print

- Delivery causes message to be perceived as more urgent
- Graphics and words but usually poor-quality reprints
- Ability to broadcast message at a reasonable cost
- Familiarity or prior understanding with audience member results in response

Types of Print (with Phone) Vehicles Available

Individual faxes	Fax broadcasting
Fax on demand	Fax cover sheet

Rules of the Road for Print Vehicles

More matter is being printed and published today than ever before . . . readers want what is important to be clearly laid out. They will not read anything that is troublesome to read, but are pleased with what looks clear and well arranged, for it will make their task of understanding easier. For this reason, the important part must stand out and the unimportant must be subdued.

Jan Tschichold, 1935

1. Less is always more. Give people enough information to catch their attention and whet their appetite for more, but not so much that they decide they don't have the time to read it.

2. Many readers skim material, so you want the important points to be eye-catching. Help readers out. Use headings, subheadings, bullets, and pull quotes. By breaking up the text and providing variety, you make the page more inviting and give the reader an immediate reason to be interested. After all, something is better than nothing!

3. People are more apt to read things they've requested.

4. With a brochure, you have three seconds to capture your reader's attention. With an unsolicited direct mail piece, you have about eleven seconds.

5. Be realistic about what you want your piece to accomplish. Give it a single goal and don't assume a single brochure can reach everyone!

6. Every photo must have a caption. Most readers read captions, so take care in writing them and format them consistently. Photo captions are read 70 percent more frequently than other copy.

7. Never use large blocks of boldface type. By emphasizing everything, you emphasize nothing.

8. Don't underestimate the visual interest of a page. If a piece looks interesting, it is more likely to be read.

9. Forty percent of direct mail's success is based on reaching the right people, and the other 40 percent is based on the "quality of the offer and who's making it."

10. Newsletters are about relationship building, not about news. The intensity of the relationship that exists between the organization and the recipient is the primary influence on the likelihood that a newsletter will be looked at—the closer the relationship to the organization, the more likely the recipient will actually read all or part of the newsletter.

11. Whether mailed or faxed, an alert must be designed so as to stand out in a crowd of print materials. Over time, recipients must recognize the look of an alert as synonymous with the need to act.

12. A press release is all about news—a "media alert" or "media update" may be used as a way to contact the media with important information that is not news. Not only must the headline grab reporters' attention, but it must also make them aware of why this is important to their audience(s).

13. Send out a short adjunct piece that highlights one or two points from a report. Since different audiences may have an interest in the report for different reasons, different points can be used for different mailing lists.

14. Because posters, billboards, and transit ads are best used to deliver a single, simple message—pared down to a few words and/or a powerful image—they are most effective when reinforcing messages or information that the viewers of these display media have received elsewhere over a period of time.

15. When printing costs are large, they're an easy target for budget cuts. Focus on reducing your total print bill rather than increasing it with the intent to lower unit cost. Send information only to those people who want it or need it.

16. Save well-designed materials that come across your desk and clever layouts from magazines or newspapers. Think about why these particular treatments grabbed your attention and use that information the next time you decide to use that type of vehicle.

17. Take advantage of every opportunity! Say something about your organization on your fax cover page, on the back of your business card, in the space on the back of a brochure that you'd normally leave blank for use as a self-mailer,[1] on the postage meter mark, invoices, and checks, on your fax header at the top of every page, even your stationery! Keep your message in front of people any way you can.

FACE-TO-FACE

✔ Face-to-face strategies can influence two different audience groups—the participants and the observers—simultaneously. For example, an organization convenes a summit at which experts present papers and discuss the latest trends in infant mortality rates. While the experts are involved in developing a consensus on the causes of and possible solutions for the problem, the press, policy makers, community leaders, or other decision makers who are observing the proceedings are made aware of the problem's existence. Indeed, this type of activity often is used by nonprofit organizations for such a dual purpose.

---

[1] Don't leave the backs of brochures blank for self-mailing. The back of a brochure is usually the second place a person looks at—after the cover. Besides, sending a brochure in an envelope has a more personal feel.

✔ Face-to-face meetings or events convey immediacy about an issue or message(s) because things happen in real time and in a shared space.

✔ When different personalities come together and interact according to a set of rules or an agenda, how an event is experienced will determine how the messages are perceived and remembered.

✔ Since it is expensive to bring people together in terms of both time and money, face-to-face programs convey the impression that "something is happening here," otherwise why would these people have shown up? Why would the organization have spent all this money?

✔ Because participants are able to read each other's body language and look into each other's eyes, they are more likely to recognize misunderstandings, listen to opposing viewpoints, and challenge their own suppositions based on the perceived sincerity of the other participant's desire to do the same. Because of this, the face-to-face program is one of the best ways to engage individuals to work through complex or conflicting attitudes, opinions, and beliefs about an issue, problem, or concern.

✔ Individuals who observe the interaction of others are less likely to be actively engaged in examining their own values, opinions, attitudes, and beliefs about the topic at hand and more likely to be analyzing what is happening between or among the participants.

✔ When participants at a face-to-face meeting or event generate enough energy and enthusiasm for action, observers who are physically present are likely to be caught up by what's happening and take action as well. For example, at a rally or demonstration, people who are on the sidelines watching often join in. Reporters covering this type of event are unconsciously influenced by the energy of the crowd and end up reporting the story (which is the appropriate action for them to take).

✔ Eye contact—one of the most direct ways to connect with another person—is instrumental in the development of trust, which is the foundation of human relationships (and thus the basis for good organizational relationships as well). Because this can only be done through a face-to-face encounter,[2] face-to-face strategies are the most effective way to build and maintain relationships either among individuals, between individuals and an organization, or between organizations.

---

[2] While videoconferencing does allow "eye contact" of a sort, it does not convey the same intimacy as eye contact made in a face-to-face situation.

Positive Attributes

- Body language
- Lends familiarity
- Greater intensity
- You can read situation and readjust more quickly
- Human touch is possible
- Real time matters

Negative Attributes

- Travel takes time and money
- Need to coordinate schedules
- Space—light, air, and so on—can influence outcome

Types of Face-to-Face Vehicles Available

Editorial board meetings	Interviews
Media tours	Press briefings
Press conference	Legislative briefings
Legislative tours	Focus groups
Board meetings	Workshops
Committee meetings	Events
Association conferences	Dinners
Seminars	Speeches
Exhibits	Tables at public spaces

Rules of the Road for Face-to-Face Strategies

1. The human dynamic—combining diverse knowledge bases, priorities, personalities, opinions, beliefs, and attitudes—can trigger unexpected positive as well as negative outcomes.

2. When considering a face-to-face strategy, carefully think about what your organization can control, what it can't control, and how the combination of these different factors will influence the end result:

   - Choosing a single audience group or individuals representing several different audience groups, their relationship to the host organization and/or issue, and how these groups interests intersect or conflict.

- The roles assigned to various individuals and/or groups—speaker, listener, reporter, facilitator, planning partner, and so on.

- The place—how convenient or inconvenient is it for the majority of participants? Is it in a city or at a remote conference center?

- The space—indoor, outdoor, or a combination? How will the room be arranged? Will there be a podium to convey formality? Will chairs be set in a circle to encourage discussion?

- The temperature and lighting.

- Acoustics—how easy is it for people to be heard without microphones? If microphones are needed, how will they impact participants' engagement?

- Seating assignments or ad hoc seating—who decides on the arrangement, since the individuals on either side of you are likely to influence your immediate involvement with the program and the information?

- The physical relationship/distance between participants and observers—how to ensure that observers do not hinder the participants' experience.

- The time commitment and how it is allocated.

- The ground rules for interaction set prior to or at the beginning of the meeting or event.

- The expectations of participants, observers, and the sponsoring organization's board, staff, and partners.

3. Always give something to individuals before they leave any face-to-face meeting or event as a take-away that will reinforce the individual's experience afterward.

4. The biggest advantage of an invitation-only event is that the organization controls the guest list (although people may choose not to come, which also influences the event's dynamics). By carefully selecting the mix of participants, an organization can advance a discussion about an issue in a structured way and ensure either that a single perspective is featured or that many viewpoints are represented.

5. In selecting a format where the interaction takes place in a certain way—for example, setting the ground rules—the organization also ensures that conflicting attitudes don't disrupt the meeting.

6. When meetings or events are open to the public, the audience is self-selected, often making it impossible for the host organization to control what messages attendees walk away remembering.

7. Many open-to-the-public meetings attract the attention of "observer" audiences—such as the press, policy makers, opinion leaders, and so on—especially if a high turnout can be assured.

8. Because the press often interprets events through the lens of "conflict," an open-to-the-public meeting to air differing opinions and discuss divergent views may be portrayed as divisive while the heart of the matter—the substantive issue—may not get any coverage at all. At the end of the day, this divisiveness may be the message the nonattending audience receives.

9. Always give people involved in face-to-face programs an opportunity to network with each other, share experiences, and reestablish or cement existing ties with individuals who are also involved in the issues.

AUDIO: TELEPHONE AND RADIO

✔ For most people, audio technologies—telephone and radio—are convenient, affordable, and easy to use; they are especially effective when working with illiterate populations.

✔ In 1997, one-third of all U.S. households had access to a cellular phone, and 65 percent used a telephone answering device—which means that most people are now comfortable talking to automated systems.

✔ Ninety-eight percent of all U.S. households own radios and 96 percent of all Americans over age 12 are exposed to radio each week.

✔ Hearing someone's voice—the timbre, pitch, and volume—conveys the emotional context within which the speaker is placing his or her ideas—something print does not afford an organization. For example, if a speaker talks with little inflection and in a regular cadence, the listener is likely to perceive what is being said as unexciting, uneventful, perhaps even boring. However, it may also be that the speaker has chosen to speak this way so as to not alarm the listener.

✔ Radio call-in shows have a higher listener recall than a tightly organized interview form, especially among regular listeners.[3]

---

[3] M. Andreasen, "Listener Recall for Call-In versus Structured Interview Radio Formats," *Journal of Broadcasting and Electronic Media*, XXIX(4), Fall 1985, p. 421–430.

✔ Audio was the first method used by human beings to tell stories and became a powerful art form within many cultures. Today's story-tellers are heard on many public radio stations weaving vivid and compelling stories as a way to help listeners work through larger concepts or understand the human condition.

✔ Audio (via the telephone) is also an excellent way to handle routine matters such as setting up meetings, reminding people of deadlines, or providing updates on pending matters.

✔ Audio is less useful when the message that needs to be conveyed relies heavily on detailed information—statistics, financial data, and the like—that needs to be easily recalled and organized by the listener in order to grasp the message.

✔ Given our increasingly mobile population, prerecorded audiotapes are seen by adherents as an easy and fast way to obtain information while getting something else done—driving to work, walking to the bus stop, exercising at the gym, and so on.

Positive Attributes

- Convenient
- Interactive
- Personal because of one-to-one contact
- Affordable
- High comfort level
- Real time matters

Negative Attributes

- Impersonal because it lacks body language/touch
- Audio only, no body language

Types of Vehicles Available

One to one	Speakerphones
Pagers	Answering machines
Cellular	Polling
Voice mail	800 and 900 numbers
Audiotext	Audioconferencing
Smart routing	Hotlines
Information lines	

Radio Attributes

- Ever present

- Easily accessible to millions

- Able to target key audiences through demographics/lifestyle information

- Simple to use

- Interactive capability

- Affordable for advertising

- Audiotapes are inexpensive to produce

- Limited format for in-depth reports of details

Types of Audio-Radio Vehicles Available

Interviews	Talk radio
Radio PSAs	Radio networks
Community calendars	Radio actualities (audio press releases)

Rules of the Road for Audio

1. Know who is listening.

   - With telephone, this is a given.

   - Radio stations attract very specific audience groups, and in-depth demographic and lifestyle information about the audience is available from the station. Ask for it, then use it to target key audience groups.

2. Know when and where listening occurs in order to deliver your message at the time and place your listener will be most open to hearing it.

   - With telephone, callers know the numbers they've called and who they expect to get at which location. If the call was not previously planned, ask whether this is a good time to talk before proceeding with the conversation.

   - According to the 1997 *RADAR Report*, 39 percent of all listening occurs in the home, while 31 percent takes place in the car and 30 percent happens either at work or via portable radios.[4]

---

[4] Statistical Research Inc., Westfield, NJ, *1997 RADAR Report*.

- From 6:00 to 10:00 A.M., 46 percent of all listening happens at home.

- From 3:00 to 7:00 P.M., 41 percent of all listening happens in the car.

3. Audiences value the intimacy, immediacy, and anonymity of talk radio and often respond to information framed in terms of advice and counseling.[5]

4. When using audio, keep your language simple and your concepts uncomplicated.

5. Articulate each word clearly.

6. Be aware of the timbre and tone of your voice. It conveys the underlying meaning of the message—it goes beyond words and colors how people interpret the message, helping them remember what was said.

7. Make sure only one person speaks at a time and, whenever possible, set rules so as to not have people "talk over" others. Whether on a conference call or talk radio, talking over or interrupting the speaker is not only difficult to listen to, it is disruptive to the message and disrespectful of the messenger.

VIDEO: TELEVISION, CABLE, VIDEOCONFERENCING

- ✔ Ninety-eight percent of all American households have at least one television set, while 89 percent own VCRs.

- ✔ Sixty-seven percent of all American households receive cable television and 26 percent have video camcorders.

- ✔ Video is a "high-impact" communication because it conveys moving images and sound, both of which can be manipulated by the producer for a highly emotional effect.

- ✔ Video and film convey two very different feelings, despite the fact that both use moving images and sound.

- ✔ In our society, video has a very high comfort level with audiences, but it is still perceived as a difficult media for producers to work in—people need to be "experts" or get very specialized training before they can produce a video of any sort of quality.

- ✔ Videos have become portable. The duplication cost for videocassettes has dropped substantially, making this an affordable medium to distribute.

[5] P. Aufderheide and J. Chester, *Talk Radio*. The Benton Foundation and the Center for Strategic Communications, 1990, p. 9.

✔ Video engages the senses of sight and hearing.

✔ Video is an excellent medium to use when working with illiterate populations.

✔ As with any medium used by nonprofits, when videos are distributed, it is usually necessary to use another vehicle—a press release, a meeting, a phone call—to get the audience to actually *watch* the video.

Attributes

- Can be interactive
- Has visual and audio cues
- Reaches millions, yet able to target specific audiences through special-interest cable channels and local programming
- Can have a blurring or numbing effect
- Images can produce visceral effects in audiences
- When combined with satellite distribution, creates a "global village"
- Brings the world—for better or worse—into our homes
- Pervasive

Types of Audio-Video Vehicles Available

TV news	Entertainment TV
Community affairs	Special-interest channels
Documentaries	Independent videos
Talk shows	Hotel closed-circuit channels
Editorial replies	Videoconferencing
Cable access	Video news releases
VCRs	Video camcorders
Long-distance interviews	

Rules of the Road for Video Production

1. Be realistic about what you want to accomplish and be very clear about the reason for producing the video. Good message development as well as selecting images that emotionally convey the message is the key to success.

2. Video is an excellent documentation tool and is probably the best medium to use when trying to capture the live experience.

3. When something is videotaped, it is perceived as having happened.

4. Video is frequently less flexible than other techniques.

5. When producing a video, be aware of potential viewers. Younger viewers will appreciate fast edits and cutaways, while older viewers may feel bombarded by the same techniques.

6. Half of video's impact comes from sound—whether speaking voices, music, or special effects.

7. Producing a high-quality video is an expensive proposition—in both time and money—even when it's done cheaply. Know why you are doing it and how you will get people to view the video before committing the resources.

8. When producing a video, consider different ways it can be used. Editing a single video in several different ways so it can deliver a message more effectively to several different audiences is a good way to leverage the initial investment.

9. Video demands excellent presentation skills.

ELECTRONIC NETWORKING: COMPUTER COMMUNICATIONS

✔ Computer communications is a two-way medium. It engages primarily the sense of sight, although Real Audio software does allow the sense of hearing to come into play occasionally.

✔ Forty percent of all U.S. households have computers in the home.

✔ Because of advances in software, it is now possible to send someone an electronic file and know that the file can be read and printed out no matter what graphics and/or sound are embedded in it.

✔ E-mail lists are an excellent way to "spread the word," because recipients often pass the message along to other lists to which they subscribe, creating a ripple effect.

✔ According to *Parents* magazine, 85.3 percent of children currently use a computer, 70.3 percent of those children under the age of 6.

Positive Attributes

• Interactive but not necessarily in real time

• Creates links to and from different information sources

- Stretches out time for in-depth discussion, deliberation
- Creates a sense of community
- Ability to broadcast messages to millions

Negative Attributes

- Tendency to communicate "off the cuff"—things are written that would never be spoken or printed
- Linking can create a "winding road" where time is lost, and not always productively

Types of Electronic Networking (Computer) Vehicles Available

E-mail	Listservs
Infobots	Usenets
Online databases	Newswire services
Desktop publishing	Desktop video editing
Multimedia: CD-ROM	Multimedia: the World Wide Web
Multimedia conferencing	

Rules of the Road for Computer-Based Media

1. Start using technology where human communication is most intense.

2. Don't just put the computer on the desktop. Most people are still intimidated by computers. Provide time and training to get people comfortable with the technology. That way you will leverage your investment.

3. Let people just starting out with computer communications experience and get used to e-mail first before introducing them to other Internet applications.

4. Before you take the plunge to set up a Web site, don't just figure out how you will design it and why you want it, but also make concrete plans for who will update the information on a regular basis. Otherwise, it may not be worth the investment in creating and launching the site.

5. Meaningful information and your communications objectives should drive the Web site design.

6. Develop a "tiered" approach to the development of information products so that it is easy to translate them into electronic publications or from electronic to print. (For more on tiered information, see Appendix C.)

7. Promote your Web site, listserv, or electronic publications just as you would promote print publications.

8. Keep things short and sweet. A screen and a half is the ideal length of a discrete section of a Web page—the actual document may be longer, but the person can jump around to the items of most interest with the use of an index. If a section gets much longer than a screen and a half, think about creating a new heading or embedding a link to another page.

9. E-mail is like print mail. It can be printed out and filed, so watch what you say in your e-mail messages.

10. Tie your electronic communications to your other communications and vice versa to extend the impact and reach of both.

11. Test your Web site with a slower modem—9,600 or 14,000 Kbps—to get a feel for the way many individuals will experience your site. Make sure the fancy graphics can be turned off on the viewer's end if desired and that the feel of the page is still clean and professional.

12. Take advantage of the interactive capability of the World Wide Web to engage your visitors in going beyond simple reading—tests, Q&A, search capabilities for the site, surveys, and so on.

ALTERNATIVE MEDIA

You might also want to consider using other types of vehicles that don't necessarily fit neatly into the five categories listed. Many of these vehicles—usually considered products to sell to raise money for an organization—could give your message additional momentum or, at the very least, reinforce it within certain targeted audience groups. Some ideas might include:

- Graffiti
- Sidewalk art
- Wearing apparel—T-shirts, hats, jackets, sweatshirts, and so on
- Bumper stickers

- Consumer products—milk cartons, soda cans, grocery bags, and the like
- Tote bags
- Buttons
- Mugs
- Banners
- Balloons
- Cash machine electronic displays (which users see while waiting for a transaction to be completed)
- The message people hear when they phone your organization and are put on hold or are being transferred to another person
- Bookmarks
- Matchbook covers

Obviously, this category is only as limited as a person's imagination and experience. While you wouldn't want to rely on one or more of these by themselves, they can help stabilize your message and have a more subliminal impact on your audience.

Resources

Our communications environment changes rapidly. Keeping up not simply with mass media studies but also with the latest developments in new technologies and what that means for the future of communications; new rules and expectations for print; research into human interaction; and studies into what shapes our values, attitudes, opinions, and actions—all of these topics and more are relevant to anyone hoping to keep up with the evolution of this environment. Because of this, the books and periodicals listed below are an eclectic sample—by no means exhaustive—of the types of information that would be useful to read "in your spare time" in order to build on the concepts outlined in this book.

Books

Ansolabehere, Stephen, Roy Behr, and Shanto Iyengar. *The Media Game: American Politics in the Media Age.* (New York: Macmillan, 1993).

Beamish, Richard. *Getting the Word Out in the Fight to Save the Earth* (Harrisonburg, VA: Center for American Places, 1995).

Bogart, Leo. *Strategy in Advertising: Matching Media and Messages to Markets and Motivations* (Lincolnwood, IL: NTC Business Books, 1990).

Broom, G. M. and D. M. Dozier. *Using Research in Public Relations: Applications to Program Management* (Englewood Cliffs, NJ: Prentice-Hall, 1990).

Cetron, Marvin and Owne Davies. *Probable Tomorrows: How Science and Technology Will Transform our Lives in the Next Twenty Years* (New York: St. Martin's Press, 1997).

Croteau, David and William Hoynes. *By Invitation Only: How the Media Limit Political Debate* (Monroe, ME: Common Courage Press, 1994).

Fetterman, David M., Shakeh J. Kaftarian, and Abraham Wandersman, eds. *Empowerment Evaluation* (Thousand Oaks, CA: Sage Publishing, 1996).

Fitch, Mark and Patty Oertel. *Getting Your Message Out: A Guide to Public Relations for Nonprofit Organizations* (Los Angeles, CA: Center for Nonprofit Management in Southern California, 1995).

Grunig, James E., ed. *Excellence in Public Relations and Communications Management* (Hillsdale, NJ: Lawrence Erlbaum Associates, 1992).

Holtz, Shel. *Communications and Technology: A Complete Guide to Using Technology for Organizational Communications* (Chicago, IL: Lawrence Ragan Communications, Inc., 1995).

Iyengar, Shanto. *Is Anyone Responsible: How Television Frames Political Issues* (Chicago, IL: University of Chicago Press, 1991).

Iyengar, Shanto and Donald Kinder. *News that Matters: Television and American Opinion* (Chicago, IL: University of Chicago Press, 1987).

McLeish, Barry J. *Successful Marketing Strategies for Nonprofit Organizations* (New York: John Wiley and Sons, 1995).

Murray, Janet H. *Hamlet on the Holodeck: The Future of Narrative in Cyberspace* (New York: The Free Press, 1997).

Neuman, W. Russell. *The Future of the Mass Audience* (New York: Cambridge University Press, 1991).

Neuman, W. Russell, Marion R. Just, and Ann N. Crigler. *Common Knowledge: News and the Construction of Political Meaning* (Chicago, IL: University of Chicago Press, 1992).

Nicholson, Margie. *Cable Access* (Washington, DC: The Benton Foundation, 1990).

O'Brien, Jodi and Peter Kollock. *The Production of Reality: Essays and Readings on Social Interaction* (Thousand Oaks, CA: Pine Forge Press, 1997).

Peppers, Don and Martha Rogers. *The One to One Future: Building Relationships One Customer at a Time* (New York: Currency/Doubleday, 1993).

Piirto, Rebecca. *Beyond Mind Games: The Marketing Power of Psychographics* (New York: American Demographic Books, 1991).

Rivers, Caryl. *Slick Spins and Fractured Facts: How Cultural Myths Distort the News* (New York: Columbia University Press, 1996).

Salzman, Jason. *Let the World Know: Make Your Cause News* (Denver, CO: Rocky Mountain Media Watch, 1995).

Schement, Jorge Reina and Terry Curtis. *Tendencies and Tensions in the Information Age: The Production and Distribution of Information in the United States* (New Brunswick, NJ: Transaction Publishers, 1995).

Schneider, Ellen and J. Radtke, eds. *Outreach TV: Creating Community Campaigns* (New York: Center for Strategic Communications, 1997).

Schudson, Michael. *The Power of News* (Cambridge, MA: Harvard University Press, 1995).

Shenk, David. *Data Smog: Surviving the Information Glut* (New York: HarperCollins, 1997).

Shoemaker, Pamela J. and Stephen D. Reese. *Mediating the Message: Theories of Influences on Mass Media Content, 2nd ed.* (White Plains, NY: Longman Publishers, 1996.)

Stauber, John and Sheldon Rampton. *Toxic Sludge is Good for You* (Monroe, ME: Common Courage Press, 1995).

Templeton, Jane Farley. *The Focus Group: A Strategic Guide to Organizations Conducting and Analyzing the Focus Group Interview* (Burr Ridge, IL: Irwin Professional Publishing, 1994).

Torres, R. T., H. S. Preskill, and M. E. Piontek. *Evaluation Strategies for Communicating and Reporting: Enhancing Learning Organizations* (Thousand Oaks, CA: Sage Publications, 1997).

Weiss, Michael. *The Clustering of America* (New York: Harper & Row, 1988).

White, Alex. *Type in Use: Effective Typography for Electronic Publishing* (New York: Design Press, 1992).

Williams, Robin. *The Non-Designer's Design Book* (Berkeley, CA: Peachpit Press, 1994).

Yale, David R. *The Publicity Handbook: How to Maximize Publicity for Products, Services and Organizations* (Lincolnwood, IL: NTC Business Books, 1995).

Yankelovich, Daniel. *Coming to Public Judgment: Making Democracy Work in a Complex World* (Syracuse, NY: Syracuse University Press, 1991).

Periodicals

There are dozens of periodicals, and every communications professional has his or her own personal favorites. Here's just a sample.

American Demographics. Cowles Business Media, 11 River Bend Drive South, Box 4949, Stamford, CT 06907.

Columbia Journalism Review. School of Journalism, Columbia University, New York, NY 10027.

Inside the Internet. The Cobb Group, 9420 Bunsen Parkway, Suite 300, Louisville, KY 40220.

Journal of Nonprofit and Voluntary Sector Marketing: An International Journal. Henry Stewart Publications, 810 East 10th Street, PO Box 1897, Lawrence, KS 66044.

Marketing Tools. Cowles Business Media, 11 River Bend Drive South, Box 4949, Stamford, CT 06907.

New Ideas in Communications. Center for Strategic Communications, 72 Spring Street, New York, NY 10012.

Public Relations Quarterly. Public Relations Quarterly, Inc., 44 West Market Street, Rhinebeck, NY 12572.

Research Alert: The Definitive Source for Research on Americans. EPM Communications, 160 Mercer Street, New York, NY 10012.

Technology for Communicators. Lawrence Ragan Communications, Inc., 212 W. Superior St., Chicago, IL 60610.

Wired Magazine. Wired Ventures, Inc., 520 Third Street, San Francisco, CA 94107.

Occasional Reports

The Benton Foundation, 1634 I Street NW, Washington, DC 20005.

Communications and Society Program, The Aspen Institute, 1333 New Hampshire Avenue NW, Washington, DC 20036.

The Gallup Organization, 47 Hulfish, Princeton, NJ 08543.

Pew Center for Civic Journalism, 1101 Connecticut Avenue NW, Washington, DC 20036.

Pew Center for the People and the Press, 1875 I Street NW, Washington, DC 20006.

The Public Agenda, 6 East 39th Street, New York, NY.

Roper Starch Worldwide, 205 East 42nd Street, New York, NY 10017.

Yankelovich, Clancy, Shulman, Inc., 8 Wright Street, Westport, CT 06880.

Index

ABOUT THE AUTHOR

Janel M. Radtke is President of Radiant Communications, Inc., a virtual consulting group that focuses on communications planning, message development, innovative information production solutions, audience research, media convergence, and the strategic application of broadcast, on-demand, and networking technologies. Building on 20 years of experience, Ms. Radtke guides organizations in the planning, implementation, and evaluation of their communications efforts through innovative training programs and direct services. Her special interest is helping groups coordinate their communications efforts with each other to create momentum for their issues. Prior to launching Radiant Communications, Ms. Radtke was the first executive director of the Center for Strategic Communications, where she helped nonprofits learn about today's communications environment. While at the Center, she developed and authored its signature publication, *New Ideas in Communications*, and its "document on demand" library, which included more than 200 practical tools and case studies. Before joining the Center, Ms. Radtke was vice president for communications at Planned Parenthood Federation of America and co-founded New York Law School's Communications Media Center. Clients have included the Robert Wood Johnson Foundation, the Independent Television Service, POV/The American Documentary, the National Alliance for Media Arts and Culture, and Indiana University's Center on Philanthropy, among others.

About the Disk

INTRODUCTION

All the blank worksheets printed in this book are provided on the enclosed disk. The worksheets are saved in Microsoft Word for Windows version 6.0. In order to use the forms, you will need to have word processing software capable of reading Microsoft Word for Windows version 6.0 files.

SYSTEM REQUIREMENTS

- IBM PC or compatible computer
- 3.5" floppy disk drive
- Windows 3.1 or higher
- Microsoft Word for Windows version 6.0 or later or other word processing software capable of reading Microsoft Word for Windows 6.0 files.

  Note: Many popular word processing programs are capable of reading Microsoft Word for Windows 6.0 files. However, users should be aware that a slight amount of formatting might be lost when using a program other than Microsoft Word.

HOW TO INSTALL THE FILES
ONTO YOUR COMPUTER

If you would like to copy the files from the floppy disk to your hard drive, run the installation program by following the instructions below. Running the installation program will copy the files to your hard drive in the default directory C:\RADTKE. To install files, do the following:

1. Insert the enclosed disk into the floppy disk drive of your computer.
2. Windows 3.1 or NT 3.51: From the Program Manager, choose File, Run.

   Windows 95 or NT 4.0: From the Start Menu, choose Run.

3. Type **A:\SETUP** and press Enter.

4. The opening screen of the installation program will appear. Press Enter to continue.

5. The default destination directory is C:\RADTKE. If you wish to change the default destination, you may do so now. Follow the instructions on the screen.

6. The installation program will copy all files to your hard drive in the C:\RADTKE or user-designated directory.

USING THE FILES

Loading Files

To use the word processing files, launch your word processing program (e.g., Microsoft Word or WordPerfect). Select File, Open from the pull-down menu. Select the appropriate drive and directory. If you installed the files to the default directory, the files will be located in the C:\RADTKE directory. A list of files should appear. If you do not see a list of files in the directory, you need to select WORD DOCUMENT (*.DOC) under Files of Type. Double click on the file you want to open. Edit the form according to your needs.

Printing Files

If you want to print the files, select File, Print from the pull-down menu.

Saving Files

When you have finished editing a file, you should save it under a new file name before exiting your program.

USER ASSISTANCE

If you need basic assistance with installation or if you have a damaged disk, please contact Wiley Technical Support at:

Phone: (212) 850-6753

Fax: (212) 850-6800 (Attention: Wiley Technical Support)

E-mail: techhelp@wiley.com

To place additional orders or to request information about other Wiley products, please call (800) 225-5945.

CUSTOMER NOTE: IF THIS BOOK IS ACCOMPANIED BY SOFTWARE, PLEASE READ THE FOLLOWING BEFORE OPENING THE PACKAGE.

This software contains files to help you utilize the models described in the accompanying book. By opening the package, you are agreeing to be bound by the following agreement:

This software product is protected by copyright and all rights are reserved by the author, John Wiley & Sons, Inc., or their licensors. You are licensed to use this software on a single computer. Copying the software to another medium or format for use on a single computer does not violate the U.S. Copyright Law. Copying the software for any other purpose is a violation of the U.S. Copyright Law.

This software product is sold as is without warranty of any kind, either express or implied, including but not limited to the implied warranty of merchantability and fitness for a particular purpose. Neither Wiley nor its dealers or distributors assumes any liability for any alleged or actual damages arising from the use of or the inability to use this software. (Some states do not allow the exclusion of implied warranties, so the exclusion may not apply to you.)